*Sharon Coursey*

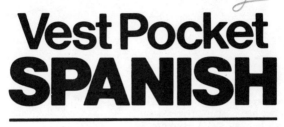

# Vest Pocket
# SPANISH

*Formerly published as: SPANISH IN A NUTSHELL*

By
## DR. SUSANA REDONDO
*Assistant Professor of Spanish*
*Columbia University*

PUBLISHED BY
**INSTITUTE FOR LANGUAGE STUDY**
**Montclair, New Jersey 07042**

DISTRIBUTED TO THE BOOK TRADE BY
**BARNES & NOBLE BOOKS**
A DIVISION OF HARPER & ROW, *PUBLISHERS*

Library of Congress Catalog Card Number: 58-8918

ISBN 0-8489-5001-1 (Paperbound)
ISBN 0-8489-5051-8 (Hardcover)

Printed in the United States of America

9 8 7 6 5 4 3 2

# GETTING THE MOST OUT OF YOUR COURSE

THE WORLD is growing smaller every day. Far-sighted people who recognize the value of speaking a second language will reap the benefits of greater business success, more traveling enjoyment, easier study and finer social relationships.

VEST POCKET SPANISH will unlock for you the treasure house of learning a language the easy way, with a fresh, new approach— without monotonous drills. Before you know it, you'll be speaking your new language easily and without embarrassment. You will be able to converse with fascinating people from other lands and read books and magazines from their country in the original language.

Much research and painstaking study has gone into the "Vest Pocket" method of learning a new language as easily as possible. This Course is the result of that research, and for the reader's convenience it is divided into several basic, closely related sections:

The KEY TO PRONUNCIATION explains the sounds of the language. Each sentence is accompanied by the phonetic spelling to help you learn the pronunciation. This method has been tested extensively and is found to be the best to enable the student to associate sounds with written forms.

The BASIC SENTENCE PATTERNS are the unique new approach to sentence construction. Here you will find sentence patterns needed in general conversation. On these basic patterns you can build sentences to suit your own particular needs.

The EVERYDAY CONVERSATIONS form the main section of this book. Here you will find a large number of situations useful for general language learning and traveling purposes. You will learn hundreds upon hundreds of conversational sentences you may need to make yourself understood. Even more important, the material is organized to provide you with a wide basis for varying the vocabulary and sentences as much as your interest and ingenuity might desire.

The OUTLINE OF GRAMMAR provides a rapid understanding of the grammatical structure of your new language. The "Basic Sentence Patterns" are closely correlated with this section to give you a quick knowledge of the language.

3

The two-way DICTIONARY of over 6500 entries includes all the words used in the Everyday Conversations and contains another 3000 frequently used words and expressions. It thus forms a compact and invaluable tool for the student.

Here are the tools. Use them systematically, and before you know it you will have a "feeling" for the new language. The transcriptions furnish authentic reproduction of the language to train your ear and tongue to the foreign sounds; thus you can SEE the phrase, SAY the phrase, HEAR the phrase, and LEARN the phrase.

Remember that repetition and practice are the foundation stones of language learning. Repeat and practice what you have learned as often as you can. You will be amazed (and your friends will, too) how quickly you have acquired a really practical knowledge of Spanish.

THE EDITORS

# TABLE OF CONTENTS

Getting the Most out of your Course                    3

Key to Spanish Pronunciation                           7

Basic Sentence Patterns                                8

Everyday Conversations                                17

  Basic Expressions                         17
  Getting to Know You                        18
  Counting                                   20
  The Clock and the Calendar                 21
  Stranger in Town                           23
  Aboard Ship                                26
  Plane Travel                               27
  All Aboard                                 29
  Going through Customs                      30
  Taxi!                                      31
  Bus Stop                                   32
  Motoring through Latin America             33
  At the Hotel                               34
  Renting a Room                             37
  The Sidewalk Café                          38
  Dining Out                                 39
  Native Dishes                              41
  Sightseeing and Amusements                 43
  Snapshots for Remembrance                  47
  Shopping with Assurance                    49
  Laundry and Cleaning                       54
  Hairdressers and Barbers                   54
  Going to Church                            55

Theater Going                                                  56
Night Life                                                     56
Exchanging Money                                               57
Communications (Mail, Telephoning, Telegrams)                  58
Tourist Information                                            61
Your Health Abroad                                             62
Sports                                                         63
Conducting Business                                            64

Outline of Spanish Grammar                                     65

  1. The Article                                     65
  2. The Noun                                        65
  3. The Adjective                                   66
  4. The Pronoun                                     68
  5. The Numerals                                    71
  6. The Preposition                                 71
  7. The Adverb                                      72
  8. The Conjunction                                 72
  9. The Interjection                                72
 10. The Verb                                             73

Table of Irregular Verbs                                       78

Useful Information for Motorists                               84

Spanish—English Dictionary                                     85

English—Spanish Dictionary                                     108

# KEY TO SPANISH PRONUNCIATION

Spanish sounds are easy to master. There are only five vowel sounds:

| SPANISH SPELLING | PHONETIC SYMBOL | DESCRIPTION | EXAMPLES |
|---|---|---|---|
| a | ah | as in *father* | *butaca* (boo-tah'kah) , armchair |
| e | ay | as in *met* | *mesa* (may'sah) , table |
| i | ee | as in *machine* | *primo* (pree'moh) , cousin |
| o | oh | as in *north* | *esposo* (ays-poh'soh) , husband |
| u | oo | as in *rule* | *duda* (doo'dah) , doubt |

Spanish diphthongs are common, but their pronunciation offers no difficulty, since each of the two vowels keeps its individual quality even though both are pronounced in conjunction *bueno* (booay'noh) good; *caigo* (kah'ee-goh) I fall; *pausa* (pah'oo-sah) pause; *miente* (meeayn'tay) mind; *reina* (ray'ee-nah) queen; *oigo* (oh'ee-goh) I hear; *feudo* (fay'oo-doh) feud.

The consonants *d, f, l, m, n, p, q, s, t, x,* and *ch* are pronounced almost as in English.

**C** is pronounced as *k* in *key* before *a, o, u,* or before a consonant and *s* as in *see* (in Latin American Spanish) or *th* as in *thin* (in Castilian Spanish) before e and i: *cada* (kah'dah) , each; *cena* (say'nah) , supper; *cruz* (kroos) , cross.

**G** as *g* in *go* before *a, o, u,* or before a consonant, and as *h* in *hue,* before *e* and *i: gato* (gah'toh) , cat; *gente* (hayn'tay) , people.

**H** is never pronounced: *hacer* (ah-sayr') , to do.

**J** as *h* in *hue: jugar* (hoo-gahr') , to play.

**LL** as *y* in *yes* (in Latin-American Spanish) or as *lli* in *billiards* (in Castilian Spanish) : *calle* (kah'yay or kah'lyay) , street.

**N** as *ny* in *canyon: niño* (nee'nyoh) , child.

**R** (as *r* in British *very*) is a trilled *r: pero* (pay'roh) , but.

**RR** as single Spanish *r,* but much more strongly trilled: *perro* (pay'rroh) dog.

**Y** as *y* in *yes: yo* (yoh) I.

**Z** as *s* in *see* (in Latin-American Spanish) or as *th* in *thin* (in Castilian Spanish) : *zapato* (sah-pah'toh or thah-pah'toh) , shoe.

**B** and **V** are pronounced alike, but they have two different pronunciations depending on their position. At the beginning of a word and after *m* or *n,* they are pronounced as *b* in *Bob.* In all other cases, they are pronounced as *v* but with the lips brought together: *bobo* (boh'boh) fool; *breve* (bray'vay) brief; *vaca* (vah'kah) cow; *vivir* (vee-veer') to live.

The **accent** of the words is indicated in the phonetic transcription of the phrases by an accent mark following the syllable to be stressed.

The rules concerning the position of the accent in Spanish are: All words ending in a vowel, in *n* or in *s* have the accent on the next to the last syllable. In all other cases the accent is on the last syllable, except when it is marked by an accent in the spelling of a word.

# BASIC SENTENCE PATTERNS

In each language there are a few basic types of sentences which are used more often than others in everyday speech.

On the basis of such sentences, it is possible to form many others by substituting one or two of the words of each of these basic sentences. The sentences selected to illustrate the basic patterns are short, easy to memorize and useful. Learning them before you tackle the main section of the book with the phrases which cover everyday needs and travel situations, you will acquire an idea of the structure of the language. You will also learn indirectly through these basic types of sentences some of the most important grammatical categories and their function in the construction of the sentences the natural way—the way they are encountered in actual usage.

Cross references have been supplied to establish a correlation between the basic sentence patterns and the Grammar section in this book. This will help you to relate the grammatical knowledge you'll acquire passively going through the sentences to the systematic presentation of the basic facts of grammar. For example, when you encounter the phrase "See 4.4" in the first group of sentences, it means that by turning to chapter 4, subdivision 4 in the Grammar section you will find a description of the interrogative pronouns and their uses.

 ## SIMPLE QUESTIONS AND ANSWERS
### (See 4.4; 4.1; 2.1-2; 4.3)

| | |
|---|---|
| **¿Quién es él?** | **Es mi padre (tío, abuelo).** |
| *keeayn' ays ayl?* | *ays mee pah'dray (tee'oh, ah-booay'loh).* |
| Who is he? | He is my father (uncle, grandfather). |

| | |
|---|---|
| **¿Quién es ella?** | **Es mi madre (tía, abuela).** |
| *keeayn' ays ay'yah?* | *ays mee mah'dray (tee'ah, ah-booay'lah).* |
| Who is she? | She is my mother (aunt, grandmother). |

**¿Quién es ese muchacho?**
*keeayn' ays ay'say moo-chah'choh?*
Who is that boy?

**Es mi hermano (primo, sobrino).**
*ays mee ayr-mah'noh (pree'moh, soh-bree'noh).*
He is my brother (cousin, nephew).

**¿Quién es el otro muchacho?**
*keeayn' ays ayl oh'troh moo-chah'choh?*
Who is the other boy?

**Ése es mi hermano mayor.**
*ay'say ays mee ayr-mah'noh mah-yohr'.*
That's my older brother.

**¿Quién es esa muchacha?**
*keeayn' ays ay'sah moo-chah'chah?*
Who is that girl?

**Es mi hermana menor (prima, sobrina).**
*ays mee ayr-mah'nah may-nohr' (pree'mah, soh-bree'nah).*
She is my younger sister (cousin, niece).

**¿Quiénes son ellos?**
*keeay'nays sohn ay'yohs?*
Who are they?

**Son mis abuelos.**
*sohn mees ah-booay'lohs.*
They are my grandparents.

**Esa muchacha alta es mi amiga. (See 4.5)**
*ay'sah moo-chah'chah ahl'tah ays mee ah-mee'gah.*
That tall girl is my friend.

**¿De veras? (¿Es verdad?)**
*day vay'rahs? (ays vayr-dahd'?)*
Is that so?

**¿Dónde está mi sombrero? (See 7.4)**
*dohn'day ays-tah' mee sohm-bray'roh?*
Where is my hat?

**Aquí está.**
*ah-kee' ays-tah'.*
Here it is.

**¿(En) dónde está su portafolio?**
*(ayn) dohn'day ays-tah' soo pohr-tah-foh'leeoh?*
Where is your briefcase?

**Está allí.**
*ays-tah' ah-yee'.*
It's over there.

**¿Dónde está su cartera (de ella)?**
*dohn-day ays-tah' soo kahr-tay'rah (day ay'yah)?*
Where's her handbag?

**Está aquí.**
*ays-tah' ah-kee'.*
It's over here.

**¿(En) dónde está el baño? (cuarto para señoras . . . caballeros?)**
*(ayn) dohn'day ays-tah' ayl bah'nyoh? (kwahr'toh pah'rah say-nyoh'rahs . . . kah-bah-yay'rohs?)*
Where's the washroom?

**Está a la derecha (a la izquierda).**
*ays-tah' ah lah day-ray'chah (ah lah ees-keeayr'dah).*
It's on the right (on the left).

¿(En) dónde está el cuarto de Juan? (See 2.3)
*(ayn) dohn'day ays-tah' ayl kwahr'toh day hooahn'.*
Where is John's room?

Está por allá derecho.
*ays-tah' pohr ah-yah' day-ray' choh.*
It's straight ahead.

¿(En) dónde está el cuarto de María?
*(ayn) dohn'day ays-tah' ayl kwahr'toh day mah-ree'ah?*
Where is Mary's room?

Está un piso más arriba.
*ays-tah' oon pee'soh mahs ah-rree'bah.*
It's one flight up.

## QUESTIONS WITH *WHO* AND *WHOM*
### (Interrogatives and Demonstratives; See 4.1, 4.3-5)

¿Quién tiene mis cuadernos? Pablo los tiene.
*keeayn' teeay'nay mees kwah-dayr'nohs? Pah'bloh lohs teeay'nay.*
Who has my notebooks? Paul has them.

¿Con quién hablaba usted? Con mi amigo Pedro.
*koon keeayn' ah-blah'bah oos-tayd'? koon mee ah-mee'goh pay'droh.*
With whom were you talking? With my friend Peter.

¿Quiénes son esos hombres? Son los amigos de mi hijo.
*keeay'nays sohn ay'sohs ohm'brays?*
*Sohn lohs ah-mee'gohs day mee ee'hoh.*
Who are those men? They are my son's friends.

¿Quiénes son esas muchachas? Son las condiscípulas de mi hija.
*keeay'nays sohn ay'sahs moo-chah'chahs?*
*Sohn lahs kohn-dees-see'poo-lahs day mee ee-hah.*
Who are those girls? They are my daughter's schoolmates.

¿Qué dijo ella? Dijo que no pudo venir.
*kay' dee-hoh ay'yah? Dee'hoh kay noh poo'doh vay-neer'.*
What did she say? She said she couldn't come.

¿En qué trabaja usted? Soy vendedor.
*ayn kay trah-bah'hah oos-tayd'? sohy vayn-day-dohr'.*
What is your occupation? I am a salesman.

¿Qué es amor? Es una cosa maravillosa.
*kay ays ah-mohr'? ays oo'nah koh'sah mah-rah-vee-yoh'sah.*
What is love? It's a wonderful thing.

¿Cuál de estos libros le gusta más? Éste.
*kwahl day ays'tohs lee'brohs lay goos'tah mahs? ays'tay.*
Which one of these books do you like best? This one.

## SENTENCES WITH *HIM, HER* AND *IT*
### (*Personal Object Pronouns;* See 4.1; 10.2, 10.4)

**Juan se lo dió (a él).**
*hooahn' say loh deeoh (ah ayl).*
John gave it to him.

**Él me lo dió (a mí).**
*ayl may loh deeoh' (ah mee').*
He gave it to me.

**Yo se lo di (a ella).**
*yoh say loh dee' (ah ay'yah).*
I gave it to her.

**Ella nos lo envió.**
*ay'yah nohs loh ayn-veeoh'.*
She sent it to us.

**(Nosotros) se lo dimos (a usted).**
*(noh-soh'trohs) say loh dee'mohs (ah oos-tayd').*
We gave it to you.

**Usted no se lo dió (a ellos).**
*oos-tayd' noh say loh deeoh' (ah ay'yohs).*
You did not give it to them.

**Démelo.**
*day'may-loh.*
Give it to me.

**No se lo dé (a él).**
*noh say loh day (ah ayl).*
Don't give it to him.

**Envíeselo (a ella).**
*ayn-vee'ay-say-loh (ah ay'yah).*
Send it to her.

**Mándenoslo por correo.**
*mahn'-day-nohs'loh pohr koh-rray'oh.*
Mail it to us.

**No se lo envíe por correo (a ellos).**
*noh say loh ayn-vee'ay pohr koh-rray'oh (ah ay'yohs).*
Don't mail it to them.

## SENTENCES ON THE USE OF *THE, AN* AND *A*
### (*The Article;* See 1.1-5; especially 1.3, 1.5)

El tenedor, la cuchara, los cuchillos y las cucharitas están sobre la mesa.
*ayl tay-nay-dohr', lah koo-chah'rah, lohs koo-chee'yohs ee lahs*
    *koo-chah-ree'tahs ays-tahn' soh'bray lah may-sah.*
The fork, the spoon, the knives and the teaspoons are on the table.

**Me compré una cama, unas sillas, un sillón y unos espejos.**
*may kohm-bray' oo'nah kah'mah, oo'nahs see'yahs, oon see-yohn' ee oo'nohs ays-pay' hohs.*
I bought a bed, some chairs, an armchair and some mirrors.

**Ellos viven en la Tercera Avenida.**
*ay-yohs vee-vayn ayn lah tayr-say-rah ah-vay-nee-dah.*
They live on Third Avenue.

**España es uno de los países más bellos de Europa.**
*ays-pah'nya ays oo'noh day lohs pah-ee'says mahs bay'yohs day ayoo-roh'pah.*
Spain is one of the most beautiful countries in Europe.

**La Habana es la capital de Cuba.**
*lah ah-bah'nah ays lah kah-pee-tahl' day koo'bah.*
Havana is the capital of Cuba.

**Ella tiene el pelo rubio y los ojos azules.**
*ay'yah teeay'nay ayl pay'loh roo'bee-oh ee lóhs oh'hohs ah-soo'lays.*
She has blonde hair and blue eyes.

**Siempre tiene las manos en los bolsillos.**
*seeaym'pray teeay'nay lahs mah'nohs ayn lohs bohl-see'yohs.*
He always keeps his hands in his pockets.

**El manejar (conducir) cuidadosamente evita los accidentes.**
*ayl mah-nay-hahr' (kohn-doo-seer') kwee-dah-doh-sah-mayn'tay ay-vee'tah lohs ahk-see-dayn'tays.*
Careful driving promotes traffic safety.

**Cuesta cincuenta centavos la libra.**
*kooay'stah seen-kooayn'tah sayn-tah'vohs lah lee'brah.*
It costs 50 cents a pound.

| | |
|---|---|
| **El es dependiente.** | **Ella es bailarina.** |
| *ayl day-payn-deeayn'tay.* | *ay'yah ays bahee-lah-ree'nah.* |
| He is a clerk. | She is a dancer. |
| **¡Qué tonto!** | **¡Qué lástima! (¡Qué pena!)** |
| *kay' tohn'toh!* | *kay lahs'tee-mah! (kay pay'nah)!* |
| What a fool! | What a pity! |

## SENTENCES USING *ANYBODY* AND *ANYTHING*
### (*Indefinite Pronouns*; See 4.6; 1.7; 10.5)

**¿Ha venido alguien? Nadie ha llegado. Nadie ha venido.**
*ah vay-nee'doh ahl'geeayn. nah'deeay ah yay-gah'doh. nah'deeay ah vay-nee'doh.*
Has anybody come? No one has arrived. Nobody has come.

¿Ha estado alguien aquí? Alguien ha estado aquí.
*ah ays-tah'doh ahl'geeayn ah-kee'? ahl'geeayn ah ays-tah'doh ah-kee'.*
Has anybody been here? Somebody has been here.

¿Ha recibido usted cartas? Sí, recibí algunas.
No, no he recibido ninguna.
*ah ray-see-bee'doh oos-tayd' kahr'tahs? see', ray-see-bee' ahl-goo'nahs.*
*noh, noh ay ray-see-bee'doh neen-goo'nah.*
Have you received any letters? Yes, I received some.
No, I have not received any.

¿Tiene usted revistas americanas? Sí, tengo algunas. Allí hay una.
*teeay'nay oos-tayd' ray-vees'tahs ah-may-ree-kah'nahs?*
*see' tayn'goh ahl-goo'nahs. ah-yee' ahee oo'nah.*
Have you got any American magazines? Yes, I have some.
There is one.

¿Tiene usted periódicos ingleses? Lo siento. No tengo ninguno.
*teeay'nay oos-tayd' pay-reeoh'dee-kohs een-glay'says?*
*loh seeayn'toh. noh tayn'goh neen-goo'noh.*
Have you got any English newspapers? I'm sorry. I don't have any.

¿Tiene usted fósforos? Lo siento. No.
*teeay'nay oos-tayd' fohs'foh-rohs (oon fohs'foh-roh)?*
*loh seeayn'toh. noh.*
Have you got a match? Sorry. No.

¿Venden leche aquí? Sí, la vendemos. Por favor, déme una botella.
*vayn'dayn lay'chay ah-kee'? see', lah vayn-day'mohs.*
*pohr fah-vohr', day'may oo'nah boh-tay'yah.*
Do you sell milk here? Yes, we do. Please give me a bottle.

¿Tiene usted dinero? No, no tengo dinero.
*teeay'nay oos-tayd' dee-nay'roh? noh, noh tayn'goh dee-nay'roh.*
Have you got any money? No, I have no money.

¿Qué comió usted? Comí queso.
*kay koh-meeoh' oos-tayd'? koh-mee' kay'soh.*
What did you eat? I ate some cheese.

¿Qué compró usted? Compré algunos vestidos y un traje.
*kay kohm-proh' oos-tayd'? kohm-pray' ahl-goo'nohs*
*vays-tee'dohs ee oon trah'hay.*
What did you buy? I bought some dresses and a suit.

¿Qué mira usted? Estoy mirando algunos discos interesantes.
*kay mee'rah oos-tayd'.. ays-tohee' mee-rahn'doh*
*ahl-goo'nohs dees'kohs een-tay-ray-sahn'-tays.*
What are you looking at? I am looking at some interesting records.

# SENTENCES ON ADJECTIVES
## (See 3.1-6, especially 3.6)

**Elena es más alta que María.**
*ay-lay'nah ays mahs' ahl'tah kay mah-ree'ah.*
Helen is taller than Mary.

**Alicia es menos graciosa que Isabelita.**
*ah-lee'seeah ays may-nohs grah-seeoh'sah kay ee-sah-bay-lee'tah.*
Alice is less witty than Betty.

**Catalina es tan alta como María.**
*kah-tah-lee'nah ays tahn ahl'tah koh'moh mah-ree'ah.*
Kate is as tall as Mary.

**Catalina no es tan alta como Ana.**
*kah-tah-lee'nah noh ays tahn ahl'tah koh'moh ah'nah.*
Kate is not so tall as Ann.

**Ana es la más alta de las muchachas.**
*ah'nah ays lah mahs ahl'tah day lahs moo-chah'chahs.*
Ann is the tallest of the girls.

**Esta calle tiene más tránsito.**
*ays'tah kah'yay teeay'nay mahs trahn'see-toh.*
This street has more traffic.

**Tomaré un poco más de carne.**
*toh-mah-ray' oon poh'koh mahs day kahrr'nay.*
I will take a little more meat.

**Por favor, tome más.**
*pohr fah-vohrr' toh'may mahs.*
Please have some more.

**No deseo más.**
*noh day-say'oh mahs.*
I don't want any more.

**No quieren permanecer más aquí.**
*noh keeay'rayn payr-mahnay-sayr' mahs ah-kee'.*
They don't want to stay here any longer.

**Ya no puede ir allá.**
*yah noh pooay'day eerr ah-yah'.*
He can no longer go there.

**La muchacha vestida de seda azul fué elegida reina del baile.** (See 3.4)
*lah moo-chah'chah vays-tee'dah day say'dah ah-sool' fooay'
        ay-lay-hee'dah rayee'nah dayl bahee'lay.*
The girl with the blue silk dress was elected the queen of the ball.

**Mi amigo, el alto, tiene un automóvil nuevo.**
*mee ah-mee'goh ayl ahl'toh teeay'nay oon
ahoo-toh-moh'veel nooay'voh.*
My tall friend owns a new car.

**La bella muchacha española no vino a vernos.**
*lah bay'yah moo-chah'chah ays-pah-nyoh'lah
noh vee'noh ah vayrr-nohs.*
The beautiful Spanish girl didn't come to see us.

# THE BASIC TYPES OF SENTENCES
## (See 10.6, 10.7)

*Affirmative:*
**Esta lección es fácil.**
*ays'tah layk-seeohn' ays fah'seel.*
This lesson is easy.

*Negative:*
**Esta lección no es difícil.**
*ays'tah lyak-seeohn' noh ays dee-fee'seel.*
This lesson is not difficult.

*Interrogative:*
**¿Es fácil esta lección?**
*ays fah'seel ays'tah layk-seeohn'?*
Is this lesson easy?

**Es fácil.**
*ays fah'seel.*
It's easy.

**¿No es grande este cuarto?**
*noh ays grahn'day ays'tay kwahrr'toh?*
Isn't this room large?

**Sí, es grande.**
*see, ays grahn'day.*
Yes, it's large.

**Le di el libro a María.** (See 2.4)
*lay dee' ayl lee'broh ah mah-ree'ah.*
I gave Mary the book.

**Se lo di a María.**
*say loh dee ah mah-ree'ah.*
I gave it to Mary.

**Se lo di a él.**
*say loh dee ah ayl.*
I gave it to him.

**Ella fué allí.**
*ay'yah fooay' ah-yee'.*
She went there.

**¿No fueron ellos allí?**
*noh fooay'rohn ay-yohs ah-yee'?*
Didn't they go there?

**Sí, fueron.**
*see, fooay'rohn.*
Yes, they did.

**Quiero ir a la escuela.**
*keeay'roh eerr ah lah ays-kway'lah.*
I want to go to school.

**Usted no quiere ir a la escuela.**
*oos-tayd' noh keeay'ray eerr ah lah ays-kway'lah.*
You don't want to go to school.

**¿De veras quieren ir a la escuela?**
*day vay'rahs keeay'rayn eerr ah lah ays-kway'lah?*
Do they really want to go to school?

**Los que estudian idiomas con discos pueden pronunciar correctamente
y aprender más fácilmente. (See 4.7; 7.1-3)**
*lohs kay ays-too' deeahn ee-deeoh'mahs kohn dees'kohs pooay'dayn
proh-noon-seeahrr' coh-rrayk-tah-mayn'tay ee ah-prayn-dayrr'
mahs fah-seel-mayn'tay.*
Those who study languages with records can pronounce them cor-
rectly and learn them easily.

**¿Quién es la dama con quien lo vi a usted anoche?**
*keeayn' ays lah dah'mah kohn keeayn'
loh vee ah oos-tayd' ah-noh'chay?*
Who is the lady with whom I saw you last night?

**Es mi tía que acaba de llegar de Europa.**
*ays mee tee'ah kay ah-kah'bah day yay-gahr' day ayoo-roh'pah.*
She is my aunt who just came from Europe.

**La muchacha con quien yo hablaba es mi novia.**
*lah moo-chah'chah kohn keeayn yoh ah-blah'bah ays mee noh-veeah.*
The girl to whom I was speaking is my fiancée.

**El muchacho cuyo padre es mi maestro, vive aquí.**
*ayl moo-chah'choh koo'yoh pah'dray ays mee mah-ays'troh
vee'vay ah-kee'.*
The boy whose father is my teacher lives here.

**Cuando ella vino, él se fué.**
*kwahn'doh ay'yah vee'noh ayl say fooay'.*
When she came, he left.

**Si Juan viene, se lo diré.**
*see hooahn veeay'nay say loh dee-ray'.*
If John comes, I will tell him about it.

**Si Juan hubiera (hubiese) venido se lo habría dicho. (See 10.3)**
*see hooahn oo-beeay'rah (oo-beeay'say) vay-nee'doh say loh ah-bree'ah
dee'choh.*
If John had come, I would have told him about.

**Cuando venga Juan se lo diré.**
*kwahn'doh vayn'gah hooahn say loh dee-ray'.*
When John comes, I will tell him about it.

# EVERYDAY CONVERSATIONS

## BASIC EXPRESSIONS

**Buenos días.**
*bway'nohs dee'ahs.*
Good morning.

**Buenas tardes.**
*bway'nahs tahr'days.*
Good afternoon.

**Buenas noches.**
*bway'nahs noh'chays.*
Good evening. Good night.

**¿Qué tal?**
*kay' tahl?*
Hello.

**Adiós.**
*ah-dee-ohs'.*
Goodbye.

**Muchas gracias.**
*moo'chas grah'see-ahs.*
Thank you.

**De nada.**
*day nah'dah.*
You're welcome.

**Perdóneme.**
*payr-doh'nay-may.*
Excuse me.

**Por favor.**
*pohr fah-vohrr'.*
Please.

**Hable más despacio.**
*ah'blay mahs days-pah'see-oh.*
Speak more slowly.

**¿Cuánto?**
*kwahn'toh?*
How much?

**¿Dónde?**
*dohn'day?*
Where?

**¿Cuándo?**
*kwahn'doh.*
When?

**Déme.**
*day'may.*
Give me.

**¿Dónde está (están)?**
*dohn'day ays-tah' (ays-tahn')?*
Where is (are)?

**Me llamo Ramón.**
*may yah-moh rah-mohn'.*
My name is Ramon.

**¿Habla usted inglés?**
*ah'blah oos-tayd' een-glays'?*
Do you speak English?

**No entiendo.**
*noh ayn-tee-ayn'doh.*
I don't understand.

**¿Cómo le va?**
*koh'moh lay vah?*
How do you do?

## GETTING TO KNOW YOU

**Tengo el gusto de presentarle al Señor López.**
*tayn'goh ayl goos'toh day pray-sayn-tahr'lay ahl
        say-nyohrr' loh'pays.*
May I present Mr. Lopez.

**Encantado de conocerlo.**
*ayn-kahn-tah'doh day koh-noh-sayr'loh.*
Very pleased to meet you.

**Mi esposa.**
*mee ays-poh'sah.*
My wife.

**Y éste es mi hijo (hija).**
*ee ays'tay ays mee ee'hoh (ee'hah).*
And this is my son (daughter).

**¿Cómo esta usted?**
*koh'moh ays-tah' oos-tayd'?*
How do you do?

**Muy bien, gracias.**
*moo'ee bee-ayn', grah'see-ahs.*
Very well, thank you.

**Tiene una casa muy acogedora.**
*tee-ay'nay oo'nah kah'sah moo'ee ah-koh-hay-doh'rah.*
You have a charming house.

**¡Qué preciosa vista tiene desde esta ventana!**
*kay pray-see-oh'sah vees'tah teeay'-nay days'day ays'tah
        vayn-tah'nah!*
What a lovely view you have from this window!

**¡Qué cuarto tan bonito!**
*kay kwahr'toh tahn boh-nee'toh!*
Isn't this a beautiful room!

**¿Ha estado mucho tiempo en el país?**
*ah ays-tah'doh moo'choh tee-aym'poh ayn ayl pah-ees'?*
Have you been in the country very long?

**Solamente diez días.**
*soh-lah-mayn'tay deeays' dee'ahs.*
Only 10 days.

**¿Cuánto tiempo piensa quedarse?**
*kwahn'toh tee-aym'poh pee-ayn'sah kay-dahr'say?*
How long are you planning to stay?

**Regresaremos en cinco días.**
*ray-gray-sah-ray'mohs ayn seen'koh dee'ahs.*
We shall return in 5 days.

**Espero que su estada sea agradable.**
*ays-pay'roh kay soo ays-tah'dah say-ah ah-grah-dah'blay.*
I hope you have a pleasant stay.

**¿Le gusta México?**
*lay goos'tah may'hee-koh?*
Do you like Mexico?

**Es un país precioso.**
*ays oon pah-ees' pray-see-oh'soh.*
It is a beautiful country.

**Espero que tenga un feliz regreso.**
*ays-pay'roh kay tayn'gah oon fay-lees' ray-gray'soh.*
I hope you have a good trip home.

**¿En qué parte de los Estados Unidos vive usted?**
*ayn kay pahr'tay day lohs ays-tah'dohs oo-nee'dohs vee'vay
        oos-tayd'?*
Where do you live in the United States?

**Vivo en Boston.**
*vee'voh ayn bohs'tohn.*
I live in Boston.

**¿Está aquí en viaje de negocios?**
*ays-tah' ah-kee' ayn vee-ah'hay day nay-goh'[see-ohs?*
Are you here on a business trip?

**No, soy turista.**
*Noh, soh'ee too-rees'tah.*
No, I am a tourist.

**¿Cuántos hijos tiene usted?**
*kwahn'tohs ee'hohs tee-ay'nay oos-tayd'?*
How many children do you have?

**He pasado una tarde muy agradable.**
*ay pah-sah'doh oo'nah tahr'day moo'ee ah-grah-dah'blay.*
I have had a very pleasant evening.

**Nos divertimos muchísimo.**
*nohs dee-vayr-tee'mohs moo-chee'see-moh.*
We enjoyed ourselves very much.

**Muchísimas gracias por sus gentilezas.**
*moo-chee'see-mahs grah'see-ahs pohr soos hayn-tee-lay'sahs.
        ah-tayn-see-oh'nays.*
Thank you very much for your hospitality.

# COUNTING

## The Cardinal Numbers

**uno**
*oo'noh*
one

**dos**
*dohs*
two

**tres**
*trays*
three

**cuatro**
*kwah'troh*
four

**cinco**
*seen'koh*
five

**seis**
*sayees*
six

**siete**
*see-ay'tay*
seven

**ocho**
*oh'choh*
eight

**nueve**
*nway'vay*
nine

**diez**
*dee-ays'*
ten

**once**
*ohn'say*
eleven

**doce**
*doh'say*
twelve

**trece**
*tray'say*
thirteen

**catorce**
*kah-tohr'say*
fourteen

**quince**
*keen'say*
fifteen

**dieciseis**
*dee-ays-ee-says'*
sixteen

**diecisiete**
*dee-ays-ee-see-ay'tay*
seventeen

**dieciocho**
*dee-ays-ee-oh'-choh*
eighteen

**diecinueve**
*dee-ays-ee-nway'vay*
nineteen

**veinte**
*vayn-tay*
twenty

**veintiuno**
*vayn-tee-oo'noh*
twenty-one

**treinta**
*trayn'tah*
thirty

**cuarenta**
*kwah-rayn'tah*
forty

**cincuenta**
*seen-kwayn'tah*
fifty

**sesenta**
*say-sayn'tah*
sixty

**setenta**
*say-tayn'tah*
seventy

**ochenta**
*oh-chayn'tah*
eighty

**noventa**
*noh-vayn'tah*
ninety

**cien**
*see-ayn'*
one hundred

**doscientos**
*dohs-see-ayn'tohs*
two hundred

## The Ordinal Numbers

**primero**
*pree-may'roh*
first

**quinto**
*kween'toh*
fifth

**noveno**
*noh-vay'noh*
ninth

**segundo**
*say-goon'doh*
second

**sexto**
*say'stoh*
sixth

**décimo**
*day'see-moh*
tenth

**tercero**
*tayr-say'roh*
third

**séptimo**
*sayp'tee-moh*
seventh

**undécimo**
*oon-day'see-moh*
eleventh

**cuarto**
*kwahr'toh*
fourth

**octavo**
*ohk-tah'-voh*
eighth

**duodécimo**
*doo-oh-day'see-moh*
twelfth

## The Fractions

**medio**
*may'deeoh*
half

**un cuarto**
*oon kwahr'toh*
one fourth

**un octavo**
*oon ohk-tah'voh*
one eighth

**un tercio**
*oon tayr'seeoh*
a third

**tres cuartos**
*trays kwahr'tohs*
three quarters

**un doceavo**
*oon doh-say-ah'voh*
one twelfth

# THE CLOCK AND THE CALENDAR

**¿Qué hora es?**
*kay oh'rah ays?*
What time is it?

**Son las diez (de la mañana)**
*sohn lahs deeays (day lah mah-nyah'nah).*
It is ten a.m.

**Son las tres y cuarto (de la tarde).**
*sohn lahs trays ee kwahr'toh (day lah tahr'day).*
It is a quarter past three p.m.

**Son las siete y media.**
*sohn lahs seeay'tay ee may'deeah.*
It is half past seven.

**Son las nueve menos cuarto.**
*sohn lahs nooay'vay may'nohs kwahr'toh.*
It is quarter to nine.

**Los días de la semana son: lunes, martes, miércoles, jueves, viernes, sábado, domingo.**
*lohs dee'ahs day lah say-mah'nah sohn: loo'nays, mahr'tays, meeayr'-koh-lays, hway-vays, veeayr'nays, sah'bah-doh, doh-meen'goh.*
The days of the week are: Monday, Tuesday, Wednesday, Thursday, Friday, Saturday, Sunday.

**Los meses del año son: enero, febrero, marzo, abril, mayo, junio, julio, agosto, septiembre, octubre, noviembre, diciembre.**
*lohs may'says dayl ah'nyoh sohn: ay-nay'roh, fay-bray'roh, mahr'soh, ah-breel', mah'yoh, hoo'neeoh, hoo'leeoh, ah-gohs'toh, sayp-teeaym'bray, ohk-too'bray, noh-veeaym'bray, dee-seeaym'bray.*
The months of the year are: January, February, March, April, May, June, July, August, September, October, November, December.

**Las estaciones del año son: primavera, verano, otoño, invierno.**
*lahs ays-tah-seeoh'nays dayl ah'nyoh sohn: pree-mah-vay'rah, vay-rah'noh, oh-toh'nyoh, een-veeayr'noh.*
The seasons of the year are: Spring, Summer, Autumn, Winter.

**Los días de fiesta más importantes son: Año Nuevo, Pascua (Florida, Pascua de Resurrección) y Navidades (Pascuas).**
*lohs dee'ahs day feeays'tah mahs eem-pohr-tahn'tays sohn: ah'nyoh nooay-voh, pahs'kooah (floh-ree'dah, pahs'kooah day ray-soo-rrayk-seeohn') ee nah-vee-dah'days (pahs'kooahs).*
The most important holidays are: New Year's Day, Easter and Christmas.

**Cumplo treinta años el diecisiete de julio de mil novecientos sesenta y siete.**
*koom'ploh tray'een-tah ah'nyohs ayl deeay-see-seeay'tay day hoo'leeoh day meel noh-vay-seeayn'tohs say-sayn'tah ee seeay'tay.*
I'll be thirty years old on July 17, 1967.

**¿Qué tiempo hace? (¿Cómo está el tiempo?)**
*kay teeaym'poh ah'say? (koh-moh ays-tah' ayl teeaym'poh)?*
How is the weather?

**Hace buen tiempo.**
*ah'say booayn teeaym'poh.*
It is fine.

**Hace un bonito día.**
*ah'say oon boh-nee'toh dee'ah.*
It is a beautiful day.

**Está lloviendo (nevando).**
*ays-tah' yoh-veeayn'doh (nay-vahn'doh).*
It is raining (snowing).

**Cae un aguacero. (Está lloviznando).**
*kah'ay oon ah-gooah-say'roh. (ays-tah' yoh-vees-nahn'doh).*
It is showering (drizzling).

# STRANGER IN TOWN

**¿Hay alguien aquí que hable inglés?**
*ahee ahl'geeayn ah-kee' kay ah'blay een-glays'?*
Is there anyone here who speaks English?

**Me he perdido.**
*may ay payr-dee'doh.*
I've lost my way.

**¿A dónde quiere usted ir?**
*ah dohn'day keeay'ray oos-tayd' eerr?*
Where do you want to go?

**¿Me entiende usted?**
*may ayn-teeayn'day oos-tayd'?*
Do you understand me?

**No, no entiendo.**
*Noh, noh ayn-teeayn'doh.*
No, I don't understand.

**Por favor, hable despacio.**
*pohr fah-vohrr', ah'blay days-pah'seeoh.*
Please speak slowly.

**Por favor, repita.**
*pohr fah-vohrr', ray-pee' tah.*
Please repeat.

**¿Qué dice usted?**
*kay dee'say oos-tayd'?*
What are you saying?

**No puedo hallar mi billetera.**
*noh pooay'doh ah-yahr' mee bee-yay-tay'rah.*
I can't find my wallet.

**¡Me han robado!**
*may ahn roh-bah'doh!*
I've been robbed!

**¡Policía!**
*poh-lee-see'ah!*
Police!

**¡Llame a la policía!**
*yah'may ah lah poh-lee-see'ah!*
Call the police!

**¿(En) dónde está la estación de policía?**
*(ayn) dohn'day ays-tah' lah ays-tah-seeohn' day poh-lee-see'ah?*
Where is the Police Station?

**Por allí.**
*pohr ah-yee'.*
That way.

**¡Auxilio! ¡(Socorro!)**
*ahoo-gsee'leeoh! (soh-koh'rroh!)*
Help!

**¡Fuego!**
*fooay'goh!*
Fire!

**Soy norteamericano**
*sohee nohr-tay-ah-may-ree-kah'noh.*
I am an American.

**Lléveme al consulado americano.**
*yay-vay-may ahl kohn-soo-lah'doh ah-may-ree-kah'noh.*
Take me to the American consulate.

**He dejado mi abrigo en el tren.**
*ay day-hah'doh mee ah-bree'goh ayn ayl trrayn.*
I've left my overcoat on the train.

**¿Cómo puedo recuperarlo?**
*koh'moh pooay'doh rray-koo-pay-rahr'loh?*
How can I get it back?

**No puedo hallar mi hotel.**
*noh pooay'doh ah-yahrr' mee oh-tayl'.*
I cannot find my hotel.

**¿Puede usted ayudarme?**
*pooay'day oos-tayd' ah-yoo-dahr'may?*
Can you help me?

**He perdido mi paraguas.**
*ay payr-dee'doh mee pah-rah'gooahs.*
I've lost my umbrella.

**¿Puede usted decirme dónde está la oficina de objetos perdidos?**
*pooay-day oos-tayd' day-seer'may dohn'day ays-tah' lah oh-fee-see'nah day ohb-hay'tohs payr-dee'dohs?*
Can you tell me where the lost and found desk is?

**He perdido una maleta.**
*ay payr-dee'doh oo'nah mah-lay'tah.*
I have lost a suitcase.

**Lleva las iniciales R. G. F.**
*yah'vah lahsee-nee-seeah'lays ay'ray hay ay'fay.*
It carries the initials R. G. F.

**¿Tiene usted alguna que corresponda a esa descripción?**
*teeay'ne oos-tayd' ahl-goo'nah kay koh-rrays-pohn'dah ah ay'sah days-kreep'seeohn'?*
Have you a piece answering that description?

**Si llega, llámeme al teléfono 11-05-55.**
*see yah'gah, yah'may-may ahl tay-lay'foh-noh ohn'say-say'roh seen'koh*
If it comes in, telephone me at 11-05-55. *seen-kwayn'tah ee seen'koh.*

## (In Emergencies)

**Está preso.**
*ays-tah' pray'soh.*
You are under arrest.

**A la delegación.**
*ah lah day-lay-gah-see-ohn'.*
To the police station.

**Deseo hablar por teléfono.**
*day-say'oh ah-blahr' pohr tay-lay' foh-noh.*
I would like to use the phone.

**Debemos llamar a un policía.**
*day-bay'mohs yah-mahr' ah oon poh-lee-see'ah.*
We should send for a policeman.

**Por favor, déme su nombre y dirección.**
*pohr fah-vohrr', day'may soo nohm'bray ee dee-rayk-see-ohn'.*
Please let me have your name and address.

**Permítame ver su licencia de manejar.**
*payr-mee'tah-may vayr soo lee-sayn'see-ah day mah-nay-hahr'.*
Let me see your driver's license.

**¿Cómo se llama su compañía de seguro?**
*koh'moh say yah'mah soo kohm-pah-nyee'ah day say-goo'roh?*
What is the name of your insurance company?

**¿Tiene averías su coche?**
*tee-ay'nay ah-vay-ree'ahs soo koh'chay?*
How badly damaged is your car?

**He perdido mi tarjeta de turista.**
*ay payr-dee'doh mee tahr-hay'tah day too-rees'tan.*
I have lost my tourist card.

**¿Puedo reponerla?**
*poo-ay'doh ray-poh-nayr'lah?*
Can I get a replacement?

**¿A dónde me lleva?**
*ah dohn'day may yay-vah?*
Where are you taking me?

**Necesito un abogado.**
*nay-say-see'toh oon ah-boh-gah'doh.*
I need a lawyer.

**¿Está herido?**
*ays-tah' ay-ree'doh?*
Are you hurt?

**¿Cuánto cobran?**
*kwahn'toh koh'brahn?*
What is the charge?

# ABOARD SHIP

**Viajo en segunda clase. Camarote número veinticuatro.**
*veeah'hoh ayn say-goon'dah klah'say. kah-mah-roh'tay
noo'may-roh vayeen-tee-kooah'troh.*
I am traveling cabin class. Stateroom No. 24.

**¿Puede usted indicarme dónde está?**
*pooay'day oos-tayd' een-dee-kahr'may dohn'day ays-tah'?*
Can you please direct me?

**Usted está en la cubierta C.**
*oos-tayd' ays-tah' ayn lah koo-beeayrr'tah say.*
You are on C deck.

**Lleve nuestras maletas a nuestro camarote.**
*yay'vay nooays'trahs mah-lay'tahs ah nooays'troh kah-mah-roh'tay.*
Take our bags to our cabin.

**¿Puedo tomar el ascensor para ir a mi camarote?**
*pooay'doh toh-mahrr' ayl ahs-sayn-sohrr' pah'rah eerr ah mee
kah-mah-roh'tay?*
Can I take the elevator to my cabin?

**¿En qué dirección está?**
*ayn kay dee-rayk-seeohn' ays-tah'?*
In what direction is it?

**¿A qué hora se sirve el almuerzo?**
*ah kay oh'rah say seerr'vay ayl ahl-mooayr'soh?*
What time is lunch served?

**El primer turno es a las doce.**
*ayl pree-mayr' toorr'noh ays ah lahs doh'say.*
The first sitting is at twelve.

**El segundo a la una.**
*ayl say-goon'doh ah lah oo'nah.*
The second at one.

**¿A qué hora se sirve la cena?**
*ah kay oh'rah say seerr'vay lah say'nah?*
At what time is dinner served?

**La cena se sirve a las seis.**
*lah say'nah say seerr'vay ah lahs sayees.*
Dinner is served at six.

**Quisiera alquilar una silla de cubierta.**
*kee-seeay'rah ahl-kee-lahrr' oo'nah see'yah day koo-beeayr'tah.*
I would like to rent a deck chair.

**¿Cuánto cuesta una silla de cubierta?**
*kwahn'toh kooays'tah oo'nah see'yah day koo-beeayr'tah?*
How much does a deck chair cost?

**Cuesta dos dólares (pesos).**
*kways'tah dohs doh'lah-rays (pays'sohs).*
The cost is 2 dollars.

**¿A qué hora atraca el barco mañana?**
*ah kay oh'rah ah-trrah'kah ayl bahr'koh mah-nyah'nah?*
At what time does the boat dock tomorrow?

**Atracaremos a las ocho.**
*ah-trrah-kah-ray'mohs ah lahs oh'choh.*
We will dock at 8:00.

**Ocúpese de sacar mi equipaje a tiempo.**
*oh-koo'pay-say day sah-kahrr' mee ay-kee-pah'hay ah teeaym'poh.*
See that my baggage is off in time.

# PLANE TRAVEL

**¿Hay un avión para Caracas?**
*ah-ee oon ah-vee-ohn' pah'rah kah-rah'kahs?*
Is there a plane for Caracas?

**¿A qué hora sale?**
*ah kay oh'rah sah'lay?*
What time does it leave?

**¿Cuánto dura el vuelo?**
*kwan'toh doo' rah ayl voo-ay'loh?*
How long is the flight?

**¿Cuánto cuesta el viaje?**
*kwahn'toh kways'tah ayl vee-ah'hay?*
How much is the fare?

**Un boleto para Buenos Aires, por favor.**
*oon boh-lay'toh pah'rah booay'nohs ah'ee-rays, pohr fah-vohrr'.*
A ticket to Buenos Aires, please.

**Deseo comprar un boleto para el próximo vuelo.**
*day-say'oh kohm-prahr' oon boh-lay'toh pah'rah ayl prohk'see-moh*
I'd like to buy a seat on the next flight.  [*vway'loh.*

**Un asiento cerca de la ventana, por favor.**
*oon ah-see-ayn'toh sayr'kah day lah vayn-tah'nah, pohr
        fah-vohrr'.*
A seat next to the window, please.

**¿A qué hora sale el autobús para el aeropuerto?**
*ah kay oh'rah sah'lay ayl ahoo-toh-boos' pah-rah ayl
        ah-ay-roh-pooayr'toh?*
When does the bus leave for the airport?

**¿Se sirve comida (cena) en este viaje?**
*say seer'vay koh-mee'dah (say-nah) ayn ays'tay vee-ah'hay?*
Is lunch (dinner) served on this flight?

**¿Cuánto pesa mi equipaje?**
*kwahn'toh pay'sah mee ay-kee-pah'hay?*
How much does my baggage weigh?

**Tiene cinco libras de exceso de equipaje.**
*tee-ay'nay seen-koh lee'brahs day ayk-say'soh day
        ay-kee-pah'hay.*
You are five pounds overweight.

**Empacaré otra vez.**     **¿Cuánto cuesta por libra?**
*aym-pah-kah-ray' oh'trah vays.*    *kwahn'toh kways'tah pohr lee'brah?*
I will repack my luggage.    What is the charge per pound?

**Se cobra doce pesos por kilo.**
*say koh'brah doh'say pay'sohs pohr kee'loh.*
The rate is 12 dollars per kilo.

**Pagaré el exceso de equipaje.**
*pah-gah-ray' ayl ayk-say'soh day ay-kee-pah'hay.*
I will pay for the overweight.

**¿Dónde está el avión para San Salvador?**
*dohn'day ays-tah' ayl ah-vee-ohn' pah'rah sahn sahl-vah-dohr'?*
Where is the plane for San Salvador?

**Allá, señor.**     **Su boleto, por favor.**
*ah-yah' say-nyorr'.*    *soo boh-lay'toh pohr fah-vohrr'.*
Over there, sir.    May I see your ticket, please.

**Tiene el asiento número 8B.**
*tee-ay'nay ayl ah-see ayn'toh noo'may-roh oh'choh bay.*
You have seat number 8B.

**Amárrense sus cinturones de seguridad.**
*ah-mah'rrayn-say soos seen-too-roh'nays day
say-goo-ree-dahd'.*
Fasten your safety belts.

**¿Señorita, llegará a tiempo el avión?**
*say-nyo-ree'tah yay-gah-rah' ah tee-aym'poh ayl ah-vee-ohn'?*
Stewardess, will the plane land on schedule?

**¿Me permite un chicle, por favor?**
*may payr-mee'tay oon chee'klay, pohr fah-vohrr'?*
May I have some chewing-gum, please?

**Señorita, me siento mareado.**
*say-nyoh-ree'tah, may see-ayn'toh mah-ree-ah'doh.*
Stewardess, I feel airsick.

**¿Tiene usted algún remedio?**
*tee-ay'nay ahl-goon'ray-may'dee-oh?*
Do you have a remedy?

# ALL ABOARD

**Un boleto para Lima.**
*oon boh-lay'toh pah-rah lee'mah.*
One ticket to Lima.

**¿Cuánto cuesta el boleto?**
*kwahn'toh kways'tah ayl boh-lay'toh?*
How much is the ticket?

**Primera clase.**
*pree-may'rah klah'say.*
First class.

**Segunda clase.**
*say-goon'dah klah'say.*
Second class.

**Viaje sencillo.**
*vee-ah'hay sayn-see'yoh.*
One way.

**Ida y vuelta.**
*ee-dah ee vooayl'tah.*
Round trip.

**¿A qué hora sale este tren?**
*ah kay oh'rah sah'lay ays'tay trayn?*
What time does this train leave?

**¿A qué hora llega?**
*ah kay oh'rah yay'gah?*
When does it arrive?

**¿Es expreso o local?**
*ays ayks-pray'soh oh loh-kahl'?*
Is it an express or a local?

**¿Está tomado este asiento?**
*ays-tah' toh-mah'doh ays'tay ah-see-ayn'toh?*
Is this seat taken?

**Boletos, por favor.**
*boh-lay'tohs pohr fah-vohrr'.*
Tickets, please.

**¿Se permite fumar aquí?**
*say payr-mee'tay foo-mahr' ah-kee'?*
Is smoking permitted here?

**El carro comedor está abierto.**
*ayl kah'rroh koh-may-dohrr' ays-tah' ah-bee-ayr'toh.*
The dining car is now open.

**¿Dónde está el baño por favor?**
*dohn'day ays-tah' ayl bah-nyoh' pohr fah-vohrr'?*
Which way to the lavatory, please?

**¿Llega a tiempo el tren?**
*yay'gah ah tee-aym'poh ayl trayn?*
Is the train on time?

**Sí, llegaremos en diez minutos.**
*see', yay-gah-ray'mohs ayn deeays mee-noo-tohs.*
Yes, we arrive in 10 minutes.

## GOING THROUGH CUSTOMS

**Abran sus maletas.**
*ah'brahn soos mah-lay'tahs.*
Open your bags.

**¿Cuántos cigarrillos trae?**
*kwahn'tohs see-gah-rree'yohs trah'ay?*
How many cigarettes are you bringing in?

**¿Trae algo que no sea objeto de uso personal?**
*trah ay ahl'goh kay noh say-ah ohb-hay'toh day oo'soh payr-soh-nahl'?*
Do you have anything besides personal effects?

**¿Dónde se hizo esto?**
*dohn'day say ee'soh ays'toh?*
Where was this made?

**¿Cuántos rollos de película tiene?**
*kwahn'tohs roh'yohs day pay-lee'koo-lah tee-ay'nay?*
How many rolls of film do you have?

**¿Dónde está su documentación, por favor?**
*dohn'day ays-tah' soo doh-koo-mayn-tah-see-ohn', pohr fah-vohrr'?*
Where are your papers, please?

**Su tarjeta de turista.**
*soo tahr-hay'tah day too-rees'tah.*
Your tourist card.

**¿Cuánto tiempo piensa quedarse?**
*kwahn'toh tee-aym'poh pee-ayn'sah kay-dahr'say?*
How long do you intend to stay?

**Espero que le vaya bien aquí con nosotros.**
*ays-pay'roh kay lay vah'yah bee-ayn' ah-kee' kohn
noh-soh'trohs.*
I hope you have a nice stay with us.

**¿Quiere conseguirme un maletero, por favor?**
*kee-ay'ray kohn-say-geer'may oon mah-lay-tay'roh pohr fah-vohrr'?*
Will you please get a porter for me?

**Maletero, por favor lleve mis maletas.**
*mah-lay-tay'roh, por fah-vohrr' yay'-vay mees mah-lay'tahs.*
Porter, please take my bags.

**Al sitio de taxis.**
*ahl see'tee-oh day tahk'sees.*
To the taxi stand.

**A la estación de autobuses.**
*ah lah ays-tah-see-ohn' day ahoo-toh-boo'says.*
To the bus station.

**¿Cuánto cobra?**
*kwahn'toh koh'brah?*
How much do you charge?

**Eso es demasiado.**
*ay'soh ays day-mah-see-ah'doh.*
That is too high.

**Le pagaré diez pesos (centavos).**
*lay pah-gah-ray' deeays pay'sohs (sayn-tah'vohs).*
I will pay you 10 pesos (centavos).

# TAXI!

**¡Taxi!**
*tah'gsee!*
Taxi!

**Lléveme al distrito comercial.**
*yay-vay-may ahl dees-tree'toh koh-mayrr-seeahl'.*
Take me to the shopping center.

**Tengo prisa.**
*tayn'goh pree'sah.*
I'm in a hurry.

**Pare en la esquina.**
*pah'ray ayn lah ays-kee'nah.*
Stop at the corner.

**¿Qué edificio es ése a la derecha (a la izquierda)?**
*kay ay-dee-fee'seeoh ays ay'say ah lah day-ray'chah (ah lah ees-keeayr'dah)?*
What's this building on the right (on the left)?

**¿Cuánto es?**
*kwahn'toh ays?*
What's the charge?

## BUS STOP

**¿Dónde se toma el autobús para Acapulco?**
*dohn'day say toh'mah ayl ahoo-toh-boos' pah'rah ah-kah-pool'koh?*
Where do I get the bus for Acapulco?

**¿A qué hora sale el próximo autobús?**
*ah kay oh'rah sah'lay ayl prohg'zee-moh ahoo-toh-boos'?*
What time does the next bus leave?

**¿Cuánto cuesta el pasaje?**
*kwahn'toh kways'tah ayl pah-sah'hay?*
What is the fare?

**¿Puedo reservar un asiento?**
*pway'doh ray-sayr-vahr' oon ah-see-ayn'toh?*
Can I reserve a seat?

**¿Hace escalas este autobús?**
*ah'say ays-kah'lahs ays'tay ahoo-toh-boos'?*
Is this a through bus?

**Los boletos por favor.**
*lohs boh-lay'tohs pohr fah-vohrr'?*
Tickets, please.

**¿A qué pueblo llegaremos?**
*ah kay poo-ay'bloh yay-gah-ray' mohs?*
What town are we coming to?

**¿Qué estamos pasando a la derecha (izquierda)?**
*kay ays-tah'mohs pah-sahn'doh ah lah day-ray'cha (ees-kee-ayr'dah)?*
What are we passing on the right (left)?

**¿Cuándo llegamos a Cuernavaca?**
*kwahn'doh yay-gah'mohs ah kooayr-nah-vah'kah?*
How soon do we arrive in Cuernavaca?

# MOTORING THROUGH LATIN AMERICA

**¿Cuido su coche, señor?**
*kwee'doh soo koh'chay, say-nyorr'?*
Watch your car, sir?

**Gire a la derecha.**
*hee'ray ah lah day-raychah.*
Turn the wheel to the right.

**Derecho hacia atrás.**
*day-ray'chah ah'see-ah ah-trahs'*
Straight back.

**Corte a la izquierda (derecha).**
*kohr'tay ah lah ees-kee-ayr'dah (day-ray'chah).*
Cut sharply to the left (right).

**¿Hay una estación de gasolina cerca?**
*Ah-ee oo'nah ays-tah-see-ohn' day gah-soh-lee'nah sayr'kah?*
Is there a gas station nearby?

**Déme diez litros de gasolina.**
*day'may deeays lee'trohs day gah-soh-lee'nah.*
Give me 10 liters of gas.

**Llene el tanque.**
*yay'nay ayl tahn'kay.*
Fill the tank.

**Gasolina de alta potencia. Regular.**
*gah-soh-lee'nah day ahl'tah poh-tayn'seeah. ray-goo lahr'.*
High octane. Regular.

**Por favor, revise mis llantas.**
*pohr fah-vohrr', ray-vee'say mees yahn'tahs.*
Please check my tires.

**¿Es éste el camino a Puebla?**
*ays ays'tay ayl kah-mee'noh ah pooay'blah?*
Is this the road to Puebla?

**Derecho a quince kilómetros.**
*day-ray'choh ah keen'say kee-loh'may-trohs.*
Straight ahead 15 kilometers.

**Dé vuelta a la izquierda (derecha) en el crucero.**
*day vooayl'tah ah lah ees-keeayr'dah (day-ray'chah) ayn ayl    [kroo-say'roh.*
Turn left (right) at the crossroad.

**Hay una desviación a seis kilómetros de aquí.**
*Ah-ee oo'nah days-vee-ah-see-ohn' ah sayes kee-loh'may-trohs*
     *day ah-kee'.*
There is a detour 6 kilometers from here.

**Se me reventó una llanta.**
*say may rray-vayn-toh' oo'nah yahn'tah.*
I have a flat tire.

**No funcionan las luces (los faros).**
*noh foon-see-oh'nahn lahs loo'says (lohs fah-rohs).*
My lights (headlights) don't work.

**¿Dónde hacen composturas?**
*dohn'day ah'sayn kohm-pohs-too' rahs?*
Where can I have repairs made?

**Por favor, mande a alguien que arregle mi coche.**
*pohr fah-vohrr', mahn'day ah ahl'ghee-ayn kay ah-rray'glay
    mee koh'chay.*
Please send someone to repair my car.

**¿Me permite tomar agua para mi coche?**
*may payr-mee'tay toh-mahr' ah'gwah pah'rah mee koh'chay?*
May I have some water for my car?

**¿Me puede llevar a la estación de gasolina?**
*may pway'day yay-vahr' ah lah ays-tah-see-ohn' day
    gah-soh-lee'nah?*
Please give me a lift to the gas station.

# AT THE HOTEL

**Hice una reservación por carta (por teléfono).**
*ee'say oo'nah ray-sayr-vah-see-ohn' pohr kahr'tah
    (pohr tay-lay'foh-noh).*
I made a reservation by letter (by phone).

**Reservé un cuarto sencillo (doble).**
*ray-sayr-vay' oon kwahr'toh sayn-see'yoh (doh'blay).*
I reserved a single (double) room.

**Deseo un cuarto con (sin) baño.**
*day-say'oh oon kwahr'toh kohn (seen) ban'yo.*
I want a room with (without) bath.

**¿Tiene un cuarto con cama doble (camas gemelas)?**
*tee-ay'nay oon kwahr'toh kohn kah'mah doh'blay
    (kah'mahs hay-may'lahs)?*
Do you have a room with a double bed (twin beds)?

**Este cuarto es muy pequeño (grande).**
*ays'tay kwahr'toh ays moo'ee pay-kay'nyoh (grahn'day).*
This room is too small (large).

**¿Cuánto cuesta este cuarto?**
*kwahn'toh kways'tah ays'tay kwahr'toh?*
What is the price of this room?

**¿Cuánto tiempo piensa quedarse?**
*kwahn'toh teeaym'poh pee-ayn'sah kay-dahr'say?*
How long are you planning to stay?

**Pienso quedarme cuatro días.**
*pee-ayn'soh kay-dahr'may kooah'troh dee'ahs.*
I am planning to stay 4 days.

**El precio por un solo día es ochenta pesos.**
*ell pray'see-oh pohr oon soh'loh dee ah ays oh-chayn'tah pay'sohs.*
The price for a single day is 80 pesos.

**Por semana hay un precio especial de quinientos pesos.**
*pohr say-mah'nah ah-ee oon pray'see-oh ays-pay-see-ahl' day kee-neeayn'tohs pay'sohs.*
For a week we have a special rate of 500 pesos.

**¿Tiene usted algo más barato?**
*tee-ay-nay oos-tayd' ahl'goh mahs bah-rah'toh?*
Do you have something cheaper?

**¿Incluye las comidas?**
*een-kloo'yay lahs koh-mee'dahs?*
Are meals included?

**¿Está incluido el desayuno en el precio?**
*ays-tah' een-kloo-eeh'doh ayl day-sah-yoo'noh ayn ayl pray'see-oh?*
Is breakfast included in the price?

**Firme el registro, por favor.**
*feer-may ayl ray-hees'troh, pohr fah-vohrr'.*
Will you register, please?

**Hágame el favor de llamar a las ocho de la mañana.**
*ah'gah-may ayl fah-vohr' day yah-mahr' ah lahs oh'cho day lah mahn-yah'nah?*
Please call me at 8 o'clock in the morning.

**¿A qué hora se sirve el desayuno?**
*ah kay oh'rah say seer'vay ayl day-sah-yoo'noh?*
What time is breakfast served?

**¿Dónde está el comedor?**
*dohn'day ays-tah' ayl koh-may-dohr'?*
Where is the dining room?

**Espero una visita.**
*ays-pay'-roh oon'ah vee-see'tah.*
I am expecting a visitor.

**Por favor, dígale que me espere en el hall.**
*pohr fah-vohrr', dee'gah-lay kay may ays-pay'ray ayn ayl hohl.*
Will you please ask him to wait in the lobby?

**Desearía guardar unos valores en su caja fuerte.**
*day-say-ah-ree'ah goo-ahr-dahr' oo'nohs vah-loh'rays ayn soo kah'hah foo-ayr'tah.*
I would like to check my valuables in your safe.

**Por favor, permítame la llave de mi cuarto.**
*pohr fah-vohrr', payr-mee' tah-may lah yah'vay day mee kwahr'toh.*
Please let me have the key to my room.

**Pensamos irnos mañana.**
*payn-sah'mohs eer'nohs mahn-yah'nah.*
We are planning to leave tomorrow.

**Por favor, tenga lista nuestra cuenta.**
*pohr fah-vohrr' tayn'gah lees'tah noo-ays'trah kwayn'tah.*
Please have our bill ready.

**Por favor, mande a un muchacho por el equipaje.**
*pohr fah-vohrr' mahn-day ah oon moo-cha'choh pohr ayl ay-kee-pah'hay.*
Please send a boy for our bags.

**Tenga la amabilidad de llamar un taxi.**
*tayn'gah lah ah-mah-bee-lee-dahd' day yah-mahr' oon tak'see.*
Kindly call a taxi.

**Lo pasamos muy bien aquí.**
*loh pah-sah'mohs mooee beeayn ah-kee'.*
We enjoyed our stay here very much.

## RENTING A ROOM

**¿Desea usted un cuarto amueblado o sin amueblar?**
*day-say'ah oos-tayd' oon kwahrr'toh ah-mooay-blah'doh oh seen ah-mooay-blahrr'?*
Do you want a furnished or unfurnished room?

**Deseo un cuarto amueblado con baño.**
*day-say'oh oon kwahrr'toh ah-mooay-blah'doh kohn bah'nyoh.*
I want a furnished room with bath.

**¿Prefiere usted un cuarto con vista a la calle o al mar?**
*pray-feeay'ray oos-tayd' oon kwahr'toh kohn vees'tah ah lah kah'yay oh ahl mahr?*
Would you prefer a room which looks out on the street or on the sea?

**Tomaré el de vista al mar.**
*toh-mah-ray' ayl day vees'tah ahl mahr.*
I shall take the one with the view of the sea.

**¿Cuánto cobrará usted, incluyendo impuestos y servicio?**
*kwahn'toh koh-brah-rah' oos-tayd', een-kloo-yayn'doh eem-pooays'tohs ee sayr-vee'seeoh?*
What price will you charge, including tax and service?

**¿Podría usted hacerme una rebaja?**
*poh-dree'ah oos-tayd' ah-sayr'may oo'nah ray-bah'hah?*
Could you give me a slightly lower price?

**Después de todo, estaré aquí tres semanas.**
*days-pooays' day toh'doh, ays-tah-ray' ah-kee' trays say-mah'nahs.*
After all, I will be here 3 weeks.

**¿Podría tener un cuarto con baño por el mismo precio?**
*poh-dree'ah tay-nayr' oon kwahr'toh kohn bah-nyoh pohr ayl mees'moh pray'seeoh?*
Can I have a room with bath for the same price?

**Viviré aquí por algún tiempo.**
*vee-vee-ray' ah-kee' pohr ahl-goon' teeaym'poh.*
I will be living here for some time.

**Tome todos los mensajes.**
*toh'may toh'dohs lohs mayn-sah'hays.*
Take all messages.

**Y cuide mi correo.**
*ee kwee'day mee koh-rray'oh.*
And look after my mail.

**Si mis amigos vienen, llévelos a mi apartamento.**
*see mees ah-mee'gohs veeayn'nayn, yay'vay-lohs ah mee*
      *ah-pahr-tah-mayn'toh.*
If friends call, show them to my apartment.

**A fines de  mes le daré una propina.**
*ah fee'nays day  mays lay dah-ray' oo'nah proh-pee'nah.*
At the end of the month, I will give you a tip.

## THE  SIDEWALK  CAFE

**¡Camarero (Mozo. Mesero)!**
*¡kah-mah-ray'roh (moh'soh. may-say-roh)!*
Waiter!

**Una cerveza, por favor.**
*oo'nah sayr-vay'sah, pohr fah-vohrr'.*
A beer, please.

**Un whisky escocés.**
*oon ooees'kee ays-koh-says'.*
A Scotch whisky.

**¿Qué jugos de frutas tiene?**
*kay hoo'gohs day frroo'tahs teeay'nay?*
What fruit juices do you have?

**Tenemos de naranja, tomate y toronja.**
*tay-nay'mohs day nah-rahn'hah, toh-mah'tay ee toh-rohn'hah.*
We have orange, tomato and grapefruit.

**Una copa de jerez.**
*oo'nah koh'pah day hay-rays'.*
A glass of sherry.

**¿Qué licores tiene?**
*kay lee-koh'rehs teeay'nay?*
What kind of liqueurs do you have?

**Un vaso de vino tinto (blanco).**
*oon vah'soh day vee'noh teen'toh (blahn'koh).*
A glass of red (white) wine.

**La cuenta, por favor.**
*lah kwayn'tah, pohr fah-vohrr!*
The check, please.

**Está incluido el servicio en la cuenta?**
*ays-tah' een-klooee'doh ayl sayrr-vee'seeoh ayn lah kwayn'tah?*
Is the service included in the bill?

**No, no está.**
*noh, noh ays-tah'.*
No, it is not.

# DINING OUT

**Una mesa para dos, por favor.**
*oo'nah may'sah pah'rah dohs, pohr fah-vohrr'.*
A table for two, please.

**¿Me permite un menú, por favor?**
*may payr-mee'tay oon may-noo', pohr fah-vohrr'.*
May I have a menu, please?

**¿Sirven ustedes a la carta o comida fija?**
*seer'vayn oos-tray'days ah lah kahr'tah oh koh-mee'dah fee'hah?*
Do you serve à la carte or table d'hôte?

**Por favor, sírvanos pronto. Tenemos prisa.**
*pohr fah-vohrr', seer'vah-nohs prohn'-toh.*
*tay-nay'mohs pree'sah.*
Please serve us quickly. We are in a hurry.

**¿De cuántos platos consiste?**
*day kwahn'tohs plah'tohs kohn-sees'tay?*
How many courses are there?

**¿Qué contiene este plato?**
*kay kohn-teeay'nay ays'tay plah'toh?*
What does this dish consist of?

**¿Qué recomienda usted?**
*kay ray-koh-mee-ayn'dah oos-tayd'?*
What do you recommend?

**Primero tomaremos sopa.**
*pree-may'roh toh-may-ray'mohs soh'pah.*
First, we'll have soup.

**Mi esposa comerá esto.**
*mee ays-poh'sah koh-may-rah' ays'toh.*
My wife will have this.

**Comenzaré con caldo.**
*koh-mayn-sah-ray' kohn kahl'doh.*
I will start with broth.

**Para el platillo principal quisiera tamales.**
*pah'rah eyl plah-tee'yoh preen-see-pahl kee-see-ay'rah tah-mah'lays.*
For the main course I would like tamales.

**Con chile, por favor.**
*kohn chee'lay, pohr fah-vohrr'.*
With chile, please.

**Sin picante, por favor.**
*seen pee-kan'tay, pohr fah-vohrr'.*
Not hot, please.

**Un limón rebanado, por favor.**
*oon lee-mohn' ray-bah-nah'doh, pohr fah-vohrr'.*
A sliced lemon, please.

**De postre quiero flan.**
*day pohs'tray kee-ay'roh flahn.*
Let me have custard for dessert.

**¿Desea beber algo, señor?**
*day-say'ah bay-bayrr' ahl'goh, say-nyorr'?*
Would you like something to drink, sir?

**Sí, un vaso de vino del país.**
*see, oon vah'soh day vee'noh dayl pah-ees'.*
Yes, a glass of native wine.

**No, nada, gracias.**
*noh, nah'dah, gra'see-ahs.*
No, nothing, thank you.

**Déme una botella de cerveza fría.**
*day'may oo'nah boh-tay'yah day sayr-vay'sah free'ah.*
Let me have a bottle of cold beer.

**Una taza de café con crema.**
*oo'nah tah'sah day kah-fay' kohn kray'mah.*
A cup of coffee with cream.

**Café solo, por favor.**
*kah-fay' soh'loh, pohr fah-vohrr'.*
Black coffee, please.

**Pan, por favor.**
*pahn, pohr fah-vohrr'.*
Some bread, please.

**Más mantequilla.**
*mahs mahn-tay-kee'ya.*
More butter.

**¿Tiene panecillos?**
*tee-ay'nay pah-nay-see'yohs?*
Do you have any rolls?

**Camarero, se le olvidó darme una servilleta.**
*kah-mah-ray'roh, say lay ohl-vee-doh' dahr'may oo'nah sayr-vee-yay'tah.*
Waiter, you forgot to give me a napkin.

**Camarero, la cuenta, por favor.**
*kah-mah-ray'roh, lah kwayn'tah, pohr fah-vohrr'.*
Waiter, the check, please.

**Creo que no ha sumado bien la cuenta.**
*kray'oh kay noh ah soo-mah'doh bee-ayn' lah kwayn'tah.*
I think you've added up the bill incorrectly.

**La revisaré otra vez, señor.**
*lah ray-vee-sah-ray' oh' trah vays, say-nyorr'.*
I'll check it again, sir.

**Tiene razón, me he equivocado.**
*tee-ay'nay rah-sohn' may ay ay-kee-voh-kah'doh.*
You are right, I've made a mistake.

**Me gustó mucho la comida.**
*may goos-toh' moo'choh lah koh-mee'dah.*
I enjoyed the meal very much.

**Con gusto recomendaré este lugar a mis amigos.**
*kohn goos'toh ray-koh-mayn-dah-ray' ays'tay loo-gahr' ah mees ah-mee'gohs.*
I shall be glad to recommend this place to my friends.

**Atienden muy bien aquí.**
*ah-tee-ayn'dayn moo'ee bee-ayn' ah-kee'.*
The service was excellent.

# NATIVE DISHES

**Cocido.**
*koh-see'doh.*
Spanish Boiled Dinner. Meat, chicken, salt pork, ham, Spanish sausages and pigs feet boiled in a pot with chick peas, cabbage and potatoes. (Regional dish, Castile.)

**Caldo gallego.**
*kahl-doh gah-yay'goh.*
Spanish national soup. Bean soup with pieces of meat, ham, Spanish sausages and vegetables. (Galicia, Spain.)

**Paella valenciana.**
*pah-ay'yah vah-layn-seeah'nah.*
Yellow rice with sea food, chicken, pork and lima beans or peas. (Valencia, Spain) [Maybe the most popular of all Spanish dishes.]

**Arroz con pollo.**
*ah-rrohs' kohn poh'yoh.*
Yellow rice with chicken.

**Solomillo asado a la parrilla.**
*sah-loh-mee'yoh ah-sah'doh ah lah pah-rree'yah.*
Grilled tenderloin, served without sauce or with many variations of sauces.

**Picadillo de carne.**
*pee-kah-dee'yoh day kahrr'nay.*
Highly-seasoned finely chopped beef and pork cooked in a sauce of olive oil, onions, capers, olives and raisins.

**Empanadas.**
*aym-pah-nah'dahs.*
Meat pie, biscuit dough filled with chopped meat (picadillo) and deep-fried.

**Chilindrón de carnero.**
*chee-leen-drohn' day kahrr-nay'roh.*
Mutton cooked in a dry sherry wine sauce.

**Guisado de riñones de ternera.**
*gee-sah'doh day ree-nyoh'nays day tayrr-nay'rah.*
Stew of veal kidney with Madeira wine or sweet sherry wine sauce.

**Codornices a la malagueña.**
*koh-dohrr-nee'says ah lah mah-lah-gay'nyah.*
Roasted quails stuffed with grapes, grated orange peel, raisins and brandy. Served in its own sauce to which brandy is added and ignited. (Málaga, Spain.)

**Pollo en cazuela con legumbres.**
*poh'yoh ayn kah-sooay'lah kohn lay-goom'brays.*
Chicken cooked in casserole with vegetables.

**Lengua guisada en pepitoria.**
*layng'gwah gee-sah'dah ayn pay-pee-toh'reeah.*
Sliced tongue or pieces of chicken served in a sauce made of white wine, egg yolks, almonds and olives.

**Pescado en escabeche.**
*pays-kah'doh ayn ays-kah-bay'chay.*
Fried or boiled fish which has been kept for some time in a sauce made of olive oil, vinegar, dry mustard, laurel leaves, green peppers, salt, pepper, olives and onions. It is served cold.

**Pescado en salsa verde.**
*pays-kah'doh ayn sahl'sah vayrr'day.*
Baked fish served in a sauce whose basic ingredient is parsley.

**Pescado relleno.**
*pays-kah'doh rray-yay'noh.*
Stuffed fish, generally red snapper, boned, stuffed with vegetables and served in tomato sauce or green sauce.

**Bacalao a la vizcaína.**
*bah-kah-lah'oh ah lah vees-kah-ee'nah.*
Pieces of salt cod fish served in an olive oil sauce with fried slices of
      bread and hard boiled eggs. (Basque country)

**Calamares en su tinta.**
*kah-lah-mah'rays ayn soo teen'tah.*
Fresh squid served in a red wine sauce and its own "ink".

**Hongos rellenos con almendras.**
*ohn'gohs rray-yay'nohs kohn ahl-mayn'drahs.*
Grilled mushroom caps filled with a paste of grated mushrooms,
      almonds, butter, onions, lemon juice and sherry wine.

**Tortilla a la española.**
*tohrr-tee'yah ah lah ays-pah-nyoh'lah.*
Omelet with potatoes (not with tomato sauce).

**Guacamole.**
*gooah-kah-moh'lay.*
Mashed avocado seasoned with tomato, olive oil, finely chopped
      onions, salt and pepper. Served as hors d'oeuvres on potato
      chips or "tortillas" (Mexican pancakes). Very popular in
      South America, not in Spain.

**Frijoles negros.**
*free-joh'lays nay'grohs.*
Black beans. Generally served with white rice. (Spanish America).

**Plátanos fritos (maduros, verdes).**
*plah'tah-nohs free'tohs (mah-doo'rohs, vayr'days).*
Fried bananas (ripe, green). These are the big bananas (plantains)
      used for cooking.

# SIGHTSEEING AND AMUSEMENTS

**¿Cómo se va a León, por favor?**
*koh'moh say vah ah lay-ohn', pohr fah-vohrr'?*
What is the way to León, please?

**Lléveme a Quito.**
*yay-vay-may ah kee'toh.*
Take me to Quito.

**Más despacio, por favor. No tengo prisa.**
*mahs days-pah'see-oh pohr fah-vohrr'. noh tayn'goh pree'sah.*
Slower, please. I'm in no hurry.

**Más rápido, por favor. Tengo prisa.**
*mahs rah'pee-doh pohr fah-vohrr'. tayn'goh pree'sah.*
Faster, please. I'm in a hurry.

¿Qué es ese edificio que estamos pasando?
*kay ays ay'say ay-dee-fee'see-oh kay ays-tah'mohs*
*pah-sahn'doh?*
What is this building we are passing?

¿Tiene un fósforo?
*tee-ay'nay oon fohs'foh-roh?*
Do you have a match?

¿Habrá buenas corridas este domingo?
*ah-brah' boo-ay'nahs koh-rree'dahs ays'tay doh-meen'goh?*
Will there be good bullfights this Sunday?

¿Cuánto me cobra por un viaje a Taxco?
*kwahn-toh may koh'brah pohr oon veeah'hay ah tahs'koh?*
How much will you charge for a trip to Taxco?

Es demasiado.
*ays day-mah-see-ah'doh.*
That is too much.

Entiendo que cincuenta pesos es suficiente.
*ayn tee-ayn'doh kay seen-kooayn'tah pay'sohs ays soo-fee-see-ayn'tay.*
I understand that 50 pesos is enough.

Muy bien, lo llevaré por esa cantidad.
*moo'ee bee-ayn', loh yay-vah-ray' pohr ay'sah kahn-tee-dahd'.*
Very well, I will take you for that amount.

¿Va esta línea al Castillo?
*vah ays'tah lee'nay-ah ahl kahs-tee'yoh?*
Does this line go to Castillo?

¿Cuánto cuesta el pasaje?
*kwan'toh kways'tah ayl*
*pah-sah'hay?*
How much is the fare?

¿Este autobús (tranvía) se detiene en el Zócalo?
*ays'tay ahoo-toh-boos' (trahn-vee'ah) say day-teeay'nay ayn ayl*
Does this bus (trolley) stop at Zocalo?
*[soh'kah-loh]*

## Bullfights

Dos boletos para el domingo.
*dohs boh-lay'tohs pah'rah ayl doh-meen'goh.*
Two tickets for Sunday.

¿Tiene usted todavía boletos de sombra?
*tee-ay'nay oos-tayd' toh-dah-vee'ah boh-lay'tohs day sohm'brah?*
Do you still have some seats on the shady side?

**No, señor, sólo tengo asientos de palco.**
*noh, say-nyohr', soh'loh tayn-goh ah-seeayn'tohs day pahl'koh.*
No, sir, I only have box seats left.

**¿Cuánto cuesta un boleto de barrera?**
*kwahn'toh kways'tah oon boh-lay'toh day bah-ray'rah?*
How much is the admission to ringside?

**¿Va este autobús a la plaza de toros?**
*vah ays'tay ahoo-toh-boos' ah lah plah'sah day toh'rohs?*
Does this bus go to the bullring?

**Taxi, a la plaza de toros, por favor.**
*tahk'see, ah lah plah'sah day toh'rohs, pohr fah-vohrr'.*
Taxi, to the bullring, please.

**Por favor, aprisa. Son casi las cuatro.**
*pohr fah-vohrr', ah-pree'sah. sohn kah'see lahs kwah'troh.*
Please hurry. It's almost four o'clock.

## Jai-Alai

**¿A qué hora comienza el jai-alai?**
*ah kay' oh'rah koh-mee-ayn'sah ayl hah'ee-ah-lah'ee?*
At what time does the jai-alai start?

**Dos boletos de diez pesos, por favor.**
*dohs boh-lay'tohs day dee'ays' pay'sohs, pohr fah-vohrr'.*
Two ten peso tickets, please.

**¿En qué fila están?**
*ayn kay fee'lah ays-tahn'?*
In what row are they?

## Lotteries

**Un pedazo de billete de lotería.**
*oon pay-dah'soh day bee-yay'tay day loh-tay-ree'ah.*
A portion of a lottery ticket.

**¿Es para un sorteo especial?**
*ays pah'rah oón sohr-tay'oh ays-pay-see-ahl'?*
Is it for a special drawing?

¿Puedo ver la lista de la lotería?
*pway'doh vayr lah lees'tah day lah loh-tay-ree'ah?*
May I see the lottery list?

Déme un número con suerte.
*day'may oon noo'may-roh kohn swayr'tay.*
Give me a lucky number.

¿Cuánto es el primer premio?
*kwahn'toh ays ayl pree-mayr' pray'mee-oh?*
How much is the first prize?

Creo que me saqué algo en la lotería.
*kray'oh kay may sah-kay' ahl'goh ayn lah loh-tay-ree'ah.*
I think I've won something in the lottery.

¿Dónde puedo cobrarlo?
*dohn'day pway'doh koh-brahr'loh?*
Where can I cash it?

¿Cuánto es mi premio?
*kwahn'toh ays mee pray'mee-oh?*
How much is my prize?

## Horseracing

¿Por dónde se va a la tribuna?
*pohr dohn'day say vah ah lah tree-boo'nah?*
Which way to the grandstand?

Dos boletos para el club, por favor.
*dohs boh-lay'tohs pah'rah ayl kloob, pohr fah-vohrr'.*
Two tickets for the club house, please.

¿Dónde puedo apostar?
*dohn'day pway'doh ah-pohs-tahr'?*
Where can I place a bet?

¿Cuál es el favorito?
*kwahl ays ayl fah-voh-ree'toh?*
Which is the favorite?

Los caballos están llegando a la barrera de salida.
*lohs kah-bah'yohs ays-tahn' yay-gahn'doh ah lah bah-ray'rah day sah-lee'dah.*
The horses are approaching the starting gate.

Su caballo gana.
*soo kah-bah'yoh gah'nah.*
Your horse wins.

## Gambling

**Hagan sus apuestas, por favor.**
*ah'gahn soos ah-pways'tahs,*
*pohr fah-vohrr'.*
Place your bets, please.

**Un dólar al negro (al rojo).**
*oon doh'lahr ahl nay'groh*
*(ahl roh'hoh).*
One dollar on black (on red).

## Carnival

**¿Va a salir en el desfile?**
*vah ah sah-leer' ayn ayl days-fee'lay?*
Will you take part in the parade?

**¿Cómo podemos salir? No tenemos disfraces.**
*koh-moh poh-day'mohs sah-leer'? non tay-nay'mohs dees-frah'says.*
How can we? We have no costumes.

**¿Por qué no compramos asientos en la tribuna?**
*pohr kay noh kohm-prah'mohs ah-see-ayn'tohs ayn lah tree-boo'nah?*
Why don't we get seats in the stands?

## Regatta

**¿Cuándo comienza la regata?**
*kwahn'doh koh-mee-ayn'sah lah ray-gah'tah?*
When does the regatta start?

**¿Puede verse desde aquí?**
*pway'day vayr'say days'day ah-kee'?*
Can it be seen from here?

# SNAPSHOTS FOR REMEMBRANCE

**¿Tiene la amabilidad de permitir que la retrate?**
*tee-ay-nay lah ah-mah-bee-lee-dahd' day payr-mee-teer' kay*
*lah ray-trah'tay?*
Would you be good enough to pose for a photograph?

**Por favor párese allá.**
*pohr fah-vohrr' pah'ray-say ah-yah'.*
Please stand over there.

**No mire la cámara.**
*noh mee'ray lah kah'mah-rah.*
Don't look at the camera.

**Dése vuelta hacia acá, por favor.**
*day'say vooayl'tah ah'see-ah ah-kah', pohr fah-vohrr'.*
Turn this way, please.

**Quisiera darle esto por haberse molestado.**
*kee-see-ay'rah dahr'lay ays'toh pohr ah-bayr'say
moh-lays-tah'-doh.*
I'd like you to have this for your trouble.

**Gracias, es usted muy amable.**
*grah'see-ahs, ays oos-tayd' moo'ee ah-mah'blay.*
Thanks, it's very kind of you.

**Lleve estos dulces a sus niños.**
*yay'vay ays'tohs dool'says ah soos nee'nyohs.*
Take this candy for your children.

**Quiero que me revelen este rollo de película.**
*kee-ay'roh kay may ray-vay'layn ays'tay
roh-yoy day pay-lee-koo-lah.*
I'd like to have this roll of film developed.

**Por favor, haga una copia de cada negativo.**
*pohr fah-vohrr' ah'gah oo'nah koh'pee-ah day kah'dah
nay-gah-tee'voh.*
Please make one print of each negative.

**Deseo una ampliación de cada fotografía.**
*day-say'oh oo'nah ahm-plee-ah-seeohn' day kah-dah
foh-toh-grah-fee'ah.*
I would like an enlargement of each picture.

**¿Cuánto tardará?**
*kwahn'toh tàhr-dah-rah'?*
How long will it take?

**Déme un rollo de película número ocho.**
*day'may oon roh'yoh day pay-lee'koo-lah, noo'may-roh oh'choh.*
Let me have a roll of film, number 8.

**Quisiera un rollo de película a color.**
*kee-see-ay'-rah oon roh'yoh day pay-lee'koo-lah ah koh-lohr'.*
I would like a roll of color film.

**Déme una docena de focos "flash".**
*day'may oo'nah doh-say'nah day foh'kohs "flahsh".*
Let me have a dozen flashbulbs.

**Un rollo de película de ocho milímetros para cine.**
*oon roh'yoh day oh'cho mee-lee'may-trohs pah'rah see'nay.*
A roll of 8 mm. movie film.

**¿Tiene película para cine de dieciseis milímetros?**
*tee-ay'nay pay-lee'koo-lah pah'rah see'nay day
        dee-ays'see-says mee-lee'may-trohs?*
Do you have 16mm. movie film?

**En blanco y negro. En rollo. En magazine.**
*ayn nay'groh ee blahn'koh. ayn roh'yoh. ayn mah-gah-seen'.*
Black and white. On a roll. In a magazine.

**El precio incluye el revelado?**
*ayl pray'-see-oh een-kloo'yay ayl ray-vay-lah'doh?*
Does the price include processing?

**¿Quiere hacer el favor de ponerme el rollo?**
*kee-ay'ray ah-sayr' ayl fah-vohrr' day poh-nayr'may ayl
        roh'yoh?*
Will you load the camera for me, please?

**El diafragma no funciona. ¿Quiere examinarlo?**
*ayl dee-ah-frahg'mah noh foon-see'oh' nah.
        kee-ay'ray ayk-sah-mee-nahr'loh.*
The shutter is stuck. Will you please look at it?

**¿Por qué se me raya la película?**
*pohr-kay' say may rah'yah lah pay-lee'koo-lah?*
Why does my film get scratched?

**¿Cree usted que debo usar un filtro?**
*kray oos-tayd' kay day-boh oo-sahr' oon feel'troh?*
Do you think I should use a filter?

## SHOPPING WITH ASSURANCE

**¿Cuánto cuesta esto?**                **Es demasiado.**
*kwahn'toh kways'tah ays'toh?*          *ays day-mah-see-ah'doh.*
How much is this?                       That is too much.

**Si me hace una rebaja compraré más cosas.**
*see may ah'say oo'nah ray-bah'hah kohm-prah-ray'
        mahs koh'sahs.*
If you make a reduction I will buy more things.

**Esta es muy grande (chica).**
*ays'tah ays moo'ee grahn'day (chee'kah).*
This is too large (small).

**Esta es muy estrecha (ancha).**
*ays'tah ays moo'ee ays-tray'chah (ahn'chah).*
This is too tight (loose).

**¿Tiene algo mejor?**
*tee-ay'nay ahl'goh may-hohrr'?*
Have you anything better?

**¿Tiene usted un ejemplar de "Esta Semana"?**
*tee-ay'nay oos-tayd' oon ay-hem-plahr' day ays'tah
     say-mah'nah?*
Do you have a copy of "This Week"?

**¿Dónde puedo comprar un diario en inglés?**
*dohn'day pway'doh kohm-prahrr' oon dee-ah'ree-oh ayn ee-glays'?*
Where can I buy an English-language daily paper?

**Deseo ver unos artículos de lana.**
*day-say'oh vairr oo'nohs ahr-tee'koo-lohs day lah'nah.*
I would like to see some of your woolen goods.

**¿Tiene esto en color más claro (oscuro)?**
*tee-ay'nay ays'toh ayn koh-lohrr' mahs klah'roh
     (ohs-koo'roh)?*
Do you have this in a lighter (darker) color?

**¿Cuánto cuesta el metro (la yarda)?**
*kwan'toh kways'tah ayl meh'tro (lah yahr'dah)?*
How much is this a meter (a yard)?

**¿Qué tiene para un niño (una niña) de cinco años?**
*kay tee-ay'nay pah'rah oon nee'nyoh (oo'nah nee'nyah) day
     seen'koh ah'nyohs?*
What do you have for a five year old?

**¿Tiene usted vestidos bordados?**
*tee-ay'nay oos-tayd' vays-tee'dohs bohr-dah'dohs?*
Do you have embroidered dresses?

**¿Cuánto cuesta ese saco de ante?**
*kwan'toh kways'tah ay'say sah'koh day ahn'tay?*
What is the price of that suède jacket?

**¿Es ésta una tela importada?**
*ays ays'tah oo'nah tay'lah eem-pohr-tah'dah?*
Is this an imported fabric?

**¿En qué país se hizo?**
*ayn kay pah-ees' say ee'soh?*
In what country was it made?

**¿Cuánto cuesta este perfume?**
*kwahn'toh kways'tah ays'tay payr-foo'may?*
What is the price of this perfume?

**No me gusta este dibujo.**
*noh may goos'tah ays'tay dee-boo'hoh.*
I don't like this design.

**¿Cuánto cuestan estos aretes?**
*kwan'toh kways'tahn ays'tohs ah-ray'tays?*
What is the price of these earrings?

**Permítame ver esa pulsera, por favor.**
*payr-mee'tah-may vayr ay'sah pool-say'rah pohr fah-vohrr'.*
Let me see that bracelet, please.

**¿Es de plata pura esta bandeja?**
*ays day plah'tah poo'rah ays'tah bahn-day'hah?*
Is this tray sterling silver?

**Enséñeme una bandeja de plata.**
*ayn-say'nyay-may oo'nah bahn-day'hah day plah'tah.*
Show me a silver tray.

**Se hacen artículos de plata al gusto, verdad?**
*say ah'sayn ahr-tee'coo-lohs day plah'tah ahl goos'toh,
          vayr-dad'?*
You make silver articles to order, don't you?

**Enséñeme un rebozo de seda.**
*ayn-say'nyay-may oon ray-boh'soh day say'dah.*
Let me see a silk rebozo.

**Me gusta el negro de rayón.**
*may goos'tah ayl nay'groh day rah-yohn'.*
I like the black rayon one.

**¿Qué largo tiene el rojo?**
*kay lahr'goh teeay'nay ayl roh'hoh?*
How long is the red one?

¿Tiene esta camisa en azul?
*tee-ay'nay ays'tah kah-mee'sah ayn ah-sool'?*
Do you have this shirt in blue?

¿Tiene usted mi tamaño en verde?
*tee-ay'nay oos-tayd' mee tah-mah'nyoh ayn vayr'day?*
Do you have my size in green?

Deseo comprar un sarape grande, para cama.
*day-say'oh kohm-prahrr' oon sah-rah'pay grahn'day, pah'rah
        kah'mah.*
I want to buy a large sarape for a bed.

¿Dónde se venden los artículos de cuero?
*dohn'day say vayn'dayn lohs ahr-tee'koo-lohs day kway'roh?*
Where is the leather goods counter?

Tome el elevador al segundo piso.
*toh'may ayl el-lay-vah-dohr' ahl say-goon'doh pee'soh.*
Take the elevator to the second floor.

Por favor llame a un dependiente.
*pohr fah-vohrr' ya'may ah oon day-payn-dee-ayn'tay.*
Will you please get me a clerk.

Quisiera ver un vestido de lino bordado.
*kee-see-ay'rah vayr oon vays-tee'doh day lee'noh
        bohr-dah'doh.*
I would like to see an embroidered linen dress.

¿Tiene usted una guayabera en mi talla?
*tee-ay'nay oos-tayd' oo'nah gwah-yah-bay'rah ayn mee tah'yah?*
Do you have a guayabera in my size?

¿Cuánto cuesta esa bolsa de cocodrilo?
*kwahn'toh kways'tah ay'sah bohl'sah day koh-koh-dree'loh?*
What is the price of that alligator handbag?

¿Es hecho a mano?                Me llevaré este cinturón.
*ays ay'choh ah mah'noh?*        *may yay-vah-ray' ays'tay seen-too-rohn'.*
Is this hand made?               I will take this belt.

¿Cuánto cuesta esta botella de ron?
*kwahn'toh kways'tah ays'tah boh-tay'yah day rohn?*
How much is this bottle of rum?

**¿Qué clase de licores tiene?**
*kay clah'say day lee-koh'rays tee-ay'nay?*
What kind of cordials do you carry?

**Me gustaría probar algo menos dulce.**
*may goos-tah-ree'ah proh-bahr' ahl'goh may'nohs dool'say.*
I would like to try something less sweet.

**Déme una caja de puros tamaño panetela.**
*day'me oo'nah kah-hah day poo'rohs tah-mah'nyo pah-nay-tay'lah.*
Give me a box of cigars in the panatella size.

**Son muy fuertes estos cigarros (puros)?**
*sohn moo'ee fwayr'tays ays'tohs see-gah'rohs (poo'rohs)?*
Are these cigars very strong?

**¿Cómo se llama esta marca?**
*koh'moh say yah'mah ays'tah mahr'kah?*
What is the name of this brand?

**Por favor empáquelo en una caja.**
*pohr fah-vohrr' aym-pah'kay-loh ayn oo'nah kah'hah.*
Please pack it in a box.

**Aquí está su bulto, señora.**
*ah-kee' ays-tah' soo bool'toh, say-nyoh'rah.*
Here is your package, madam.

**Mándemelo a mi hotel, por favor.**
*mahn'day-may-loh ah mee oh-tayl', pohr fah-vohrr'.*
Send it to my hotel, please.

**Por favor, déme una factura para esta compra.**
*pohr fah-vohrr' day'may oo'nah fahk-too'rah pah'rah
ays'tah kohm'prah.*
Please let me have a sales slip for this purchase.

**No deje de enviármelo por correo inmediatamente.**
*noh-day'hay day ayn-vee-ahr'may-loh pohr koh-ray'oh
een-may-dee-ah-tah-mayn'tay.*
Be sure to mail it immediately.

**Mi dirección es Paseo de la Reforma No. 15.**
*mee dee-rayk-see-ohn' ays pah-say'oh day lah ray-fohr'mah noo'may-roh*
My address is 15 Paseo de la Reforma.                    [keen'say.

## LAUNDRY AND CLEANING

**Por favor, lave este vestido.**
*pohr fah-vohrr', lah'vay ays'tay vays-tee'doh.*
Please wash this dress.

**Sin almidón, por favor.**
*seen ahl-mee-dohn' pohr fah-vohrr'.*
Without starch, please.

**Quiero este traje lavado en seco.**
*kee-ay'roh ays'tay trah'hay lah-vah-doh ayn say'koh.*
I want this suit dry cleaned.

**¿Cuándo estará listo?**
*kwahn-doh ays-tah-rah' lees'toh?*
When can you have it ready?

**Lo necesito mañana.**
*loh nay-say-see'toh ma-nyah'nah.*
I must have it tomorrow.

**Por favor, planche estos pantalones.**
*pohr fah-vohrr' plahn'chay ays'tohs pahn-tah-loh'nays.*
Please press these trousers.

**Está roto. ¿Puede arreglarlo?**
*ays-tah' roh'toh pway'day ah-ray-glahr'loh?*
This is torn. Can you mend it?

## HAIRDRESSERS AND BARBERS

**Deseo un corte de pelo a las once.**
*day-say'-oh oon kohr'tay day pay'loh ah lahs ohn'say.*
I'd like to have a haircut at 11 o'clock.

**Deseo una cita para manicure.**
*day-say' oh oo'nah see'tah pah'rah mah-nee-kee-oor'.*
I would like to make an appointment for a manicure.

**¿A qué hora puede recibirme para un champú?**
*ah kay or'rah pway'day ray-see-beer'may pah'rah oon chahm-poo'?*
What time can you take me for a shampoo?

**Un ligero corte, por favor.**
*oon lee-hay'roh kohr'tay pohr fah-vohrr'.*
A trim, please.

**Un corte a cepillo.**
*oon kohr'tay ah say-pee'yoh.*
A crew cut.

**No me corte mucho arriba.**
*noh may kohr'tay moo'choh ah-ree'bah.*
Not too much off the top.

**Más corto, por favor.**
*mahs kohr'toh, pohr fah-vohrr'.*
Make it shorter, please.

# GOING TO CHURCH

**Quisiera ir a la iglesia.**
*kee-seeay'rah eerr ah lah ee-glay'seeah.*
I would like to go to church.

**¿En dónde está la iglesia (más cercana)?**
*ayn dohn'day ays-tah' lah ee-glay'seeah (mas' sayrr-kah'nah)?*
Where is the (nearest) church?

**¿En dónde está la Catedral?**
*ayn dohn'day ays-tah' lah kah-tay-drahl'?*
Where is the cathedral?

**¿En dónde está la sinagoga?**
*ayn dohn'day ays-tah' lah see-nah-goh'gah?*
Where is the synagogue?

**¿Qué clase de iglesia es ésta?**
*kay klah'say day ee-glay'seeah ays ays'tah?*
What kind of a church is this?

**Una iglesia católica.**
*oo'nah ee-glay'seeah kah-toh'lee-kah.*
A Catholic church.

**Una iglesia protestante.**
*oo'nah ee-glay'seeah proh-tays-tahn'tay.*
A Protestant church.

**¿A qué hora empieza la misa?**
*ah kay oh'rah aym-peeay'sah lah mee'sah?*
At what time does the mass start?

**¿Qué iglesia celebra los oficios en inglés?**
*kay ee-glay'seeah say-lay brrah lohs oh-fee'seeohs ayn een-glays'?*
What church holds service in English?

**¿Podemos asistir a este oficio?**
*poh-day'mohs ah-sees-teerr' ah ays'tay oh-fee'seeoh?*
May we attend this service?

**Quisiera ver a un ministro (sacerdote, rabí).**
*kee-seeay'rah vayrr' ah oon mee-nees'trroh (sah-sayrr-doh'tay, rrah-bee').*
I would like to see a minister (priest, rabbi).

## THEATER GOING

**Desearía dos billetes para mañana.**
*day-say-ah-ree'ah dohs bee-yay'tays pah'rah mah-nyah'nah.*
I should like two tickets for tomorrow.

**¿Tiene usted asientos para esta noche?**
*teeay'nay oos-tayd' ah-seeayn'tohs pah'rah ays'tah noh'chay?*
Have you any seats for tonight?

**¿En dónde están los asientos?**
*ayn dohn'day ays-tahn' lohs ah-seeayn'tohs?*
Where are the seats located?

**¿Puede usted mostrarme un plano de los asientos del teatro?**
*pooay'day oos-tayd' mohs-trahrr'may oon plah-noh day lohs ah-seeayn'tohs dayl tay-ah'troh?*
  Can you show me a seating plan of the theater?

**Por favor, deme dos butacas (asientos de platea, palco, galería).**
*pohr fah-vohrr' day-may dohs boo-tah'kahs (ah-seeayn'tohs day plah-tay'ah, pahl'koh, gah-lay-ree'ah).*
Please let me have two orchestra (mezzanine, box, balcony) seats.

**¿A qué hora empieza la función?**
*ah kay oh'rah aym-peeay'sah lah foon-seeohn'?*
At what time does the performance start?

## NIGHT LIFE

**Deseo visitar algunos cabarets.**
*day-say'oh vee-see-tahr' ahl-goo'nohs kah-bah-rayts'.*
I want to visit several night clubs.

**Me gustaría ver algunas buenas funciones.**
*may goo-stah-ree'ah vayrr' ahl-goo'nahs booay'nahs foon-seeoh'nays.*
I would like to see some good floor shows.

¿Qué sitios recomienda usted?
*kay see'teeohs ray-koh-meeayn'dah oos-tayd'?*
What places do you recommend?

¿Son muy caros?
*sohn mooee kah-rohs?*
Are they very expensive?

¿Cobran por la admisión?
*koh'brahn pohr lah ahd-mee-seeohn'?*
Is there a cover charge?

¿Cobran por alguna otra cosa?
*koh'brahn pohr ahl-goo'nah oh'trah koh'sah?*
Are there any other charges?

¿A qué hora comienza la función?
*ah kay oh'rah koh-meeayn'sah lah foon-seeohn'?*
What time does the floor show start?

Hay una equivocación en la cuenta.
*ahee oo'nah ay-kee-voh-kah-seeohn' ayn lah kwayn'tah.*
There is an error in the bill.

Por favor, haga corregir la cuenta.
*pohr fah-vohrr', ah'gah koh-rray-heer' lah kwayn'tah.*
Please see that my bill is corrected.

## EXCHANGING MONEY

Deseo cambiar este cheque de viajero.
*day-say'oh kahm-bee-ahr' ays'tay chay'kay day
vee-ah-hey'roh.*
I should like to cash this travelers check.

¿Me puede dar pesos por este billete de diez dólares?
*may pooay'day dahr pay'sohs pohr ays'tay bee-yay'tay day deeays'
doh'lah-rays?*
May I have pesos for this ten dollar bill?

¿Dónde puedo comprar un giro bancario?
*dohn'day pway'doh kohm-prahr' oon hee'roh
bahn-kah'ree-oh?*
Where can I buy a bank draft?

En la siguiente ventanilla.
*ayn lah see-ghee-ayn'tay vayn-tah-nee'yah.*
At the next window.

# COMMUNICATIONS

## Post Office

**¿Dónde está el correo?**
*dohn'day ays-tah' ayl koh-ray'oh?*
Where is the post office?

**¿Hasta qué hora está abierto?**
*ahs'tah kay oh'rah ays-tah' ah-bee-ayr'toh?*
Until what time is it open?

**Se cierra a las cinco.**
*say see-ay'rah ah lahs seen'koh.*
It closes at five o'clock.

**¿Dónde puedo comprar unos sellos?**
*dohn'day pway'doh kohm-prahr' oo'nohs say'yohs?*
Where can I buy some stamps?

**En la ventanilla número 4.**
*any lah vayn-tah-nee'yah noo'may-roh kooah'troh.*
At window number 4.

**Déme un sello aéreo, por favor.**
*day'may oon say'yoh ah-ay'ray-oh pohr fah-vohrr'.*
Let me have an airmail stamp, please.

**Quiero enviar ésta entrega inmediata.**
*kee'ay'roh ayn-vee'ahr' ays'tah ayn-tray'-gah*
        *een-may-dee-ah'tah.*
I want to send this special delivery.

**¿Cuánto es el franqueo de esta carta?**
*kwahn'toh ays ayl frahn-kay'oh day ays'tah kahr'tah?*
How much postage do I need on this letter?

**Deseo certificar esta carta.**
*day-say'oh sayr-tee-fee-kahr' ays'tah kahr'tah.*
I would like to register this letter.

**¿Puedo asegurar este bulto?**
*pway'doh ah-say-goo-rahr' ays'tay bool'toh?*
May I insure this parcel?

**¿Qué contiene?**
*kay kohn-tee-ay'nay?*
What does it contain?

**Libros e impresos.**
*lee'brohs ay eem-pray'sohs.*
Books and printed matter.

**Guarde mi correspondencia hasta que yo venga.**
*gwahr'day mee koh-rays-pohn-dayn'seeah ahs'tah kay yoh vayn'gah.*
Hold my mail until I call for it.

**Por favor mande mi correspondencia a Nueva York.**
*pohr fah-vorr' mahn'day mee koh-rays-pohn-dayn'seeah ah nooay'vah* [yohrk'.]
Please forward my mail to New York.

**No se moleste en mandarme revistas y periódicos.**
*noh say moh-lays'tay ayn mahn-dahr'may ray-vees'tahs ee pay-ree-oh'dee-kohs.*
Don't bother to send magazines and newspapers.

## Telephoning

**¿Dónde está el teléfono más cercano?**
*dohn'day ays-tah' ayl tay-lay'foh-noh mahs sayr-kah'noh?*
Where is the nearest telephone?

**Oigo, habla Roberto.**
*ohee'goh, ah'blah roh-bayr'toh.*
Hello, this is Robert calling.

**¿Está Luis allí?**
*ays-tah' looees' ah-yee'?*
Is Louis there?

**No está.**
*noh ays-tah'.*
He is not in.

**No cuelgue, por favor. Lo llamaré.**
*noh kwayl'gay, pohr fah-vohrr'. loh yah-mah-ray'.*
Hold the wire, please. I'll put him on.

**¿Puedo dejar un recado?**
*pway'doh day-hahr' oon ray-kah'doh?*
May I leave a message, please?

**¿A qué hora lo espera?**
*ah kay oh'rah loh ays-pay'rah?*
When is he expected?

**Deseo hacer una llamada de larga distancia.**
*day-say'oh ah-sayr' oo'nah yah-mah'dah day lahr'gah dees-tahn'seeah.*
I want to make a long distance call.

**Deseo llamar a Chicago a las tres de la tarde.**
*day-say'oh yah-mahr' ah chee-kah'goh ah lahs trays day lah tahr'day.*
I would like to call Chicago at three o'clock.

**¿Cuánto cuesta una llamada a Nueva York?**
*kwahn'toh kways'tah oo'nah yah-mah'dah ah nway'vah yohrk?*
How much is a call to New York?

**Es una llamada de teléfono a teléfono.**
*ays oo'nah yah-mah'dah day tay-lay'foh-noh ah tay-lay'foh- noh.*
This is a station-to-station call.

**Lo siento. Todas las líneas están ocupadas.**
*loh see-ayn'toh toh'dahs lahs lee'nay-ahs ays-tahn' oh-koo-
        pah'-dahs.*
I'm sorry. All the lines are busy.

**Dígale que el señor Cervantes está llamando de México.**
*dee'gah-lay kay ayl say-nyohr sayr-vahn'tays ays-tah' yah-mahn'doh day
        may'hee-koh*
Tell him Mr. Cervantes is calling from Mexico.

**Avíseme cuando terminen los tres minutos.**
*ah-vee'say-may kwahn'doh tayr-mee'nayn lohs trays
        mee-noo'tohs.*
Signal me when the three minutes are over.

**Por favor no interrumpa.**
*pohr fah-vohrr' noh een-tay-room'pah.*
Please do not interrupt.

## Telegrams and Cables

**Deseo mandar un telegrama.**
*day-say'oh mahn-dahr' oon tay-lay-grah'mah.*
I want to send a telegram.

**Por favor, déme una hoja para escribir un cablegrama.**
*pohr fah-vohr', day'may oo'nah oh'jah pah'rah ays-cree-beer'
        oon kah-blay-grah'mah.*
Please give me a blank for a foreign telegram.

**¿Cuánto cuesta cada palabra?**
*kwahn'toh kways'tah kah'dah pah-lah'brah?*
What is the rate per word?

**Tiene aquí más de diez palabras.**
*tee-ay'nay ah-kee' mahs day dee-ays' pah-lah'-brahs.*
You have more than ten words here.

**Pagaré la diferencia.**
*pah-gah-ray' lah dee-fay-rayn'see-ah.*
I shall pay for the difference.

# TOURIST INFORMATION

**¿En dónde está la oficina de turismo más cercana?**
*ayn dohn'day ays-tah' lah of-fee-see'nah day too-rees'moh mahs'*
*sayr-kah'nah?*
Where is the nearest tourist office?

**¿Cuál es el próximo autobús para La Habana?**
*kwahl' ays ayl proh'gzee-moh ahoo-toh-boos'pah'rah lah ah-van-nah?*
What is the next bus for Havana?

**¿Qué plato regional recomienda usted?**
*kay plah'toh ray-heeoh-nahl' ray-koh-meeayn'da oos-tayd'?*
What local food do you recommend?

**Deseo visitar un lugar en que no haya turistas.**
*day-say'oh vee-see-tahr' oon loo-gahr' ayn kay noh ay'yah too-rees'tahs.*
I wish to visit a place where there are no tourists.

**Tengo muchos elegidos. Por ejemplo Alvarado.**
*tayn'goh moo'chohs ay-lay-hee'dohs. pohr ay-haym'ploh ahl-vah-rah'*
I have many choices. For example, there is Alvarado.          *[doh.*

**¿Está esta ciudad fuera de los caminos concurridos?**
*ays-tah' ays'tah seeoo-dahd' fooay'rah day lohs kah-mee'nohs*
*kohn-koo-rree'dohs?*
Is this town off the beaten track?

**Sí, así es. (Sí, muy cierto).**
*see, as-see' ays. (see, mooee seeayr'toh).*
Yes, very much.

**¿Es difícil llegar a ese pueblo?**
*ays dee-fee'seel yay-gahr ah ay'say pooay'bloh?*
Is it difficult to reach that village?

**No, los autobuses pasan a menudo.**
*noh, lohs ahoo-toh-boo'says pah'sahn ah may-noo'doh.*
No, there is frequent bus service.

**¿Tienen allí un hotel bueno y barato?**
*teeay'nayn ah-yee' oon oh-tayl' booay'noh ee bah-rah'toh?*
Does it have a good, inexpensive hotel?

**Seguro. Recomendamos el Hotel Vista Hermosa.**
*say-goo'roh. ray-kho-mayn-dah'mohs ayl oh-tayl' vees'tah ayr-moh'sah.*
Certainly. We recommend the Hotel Vista Hermosa.

## YOUR HEALTH ABROAD

**No me siento bien.**
*noh may see-ayn'toh bee-ayn'.*
I don't feel well.

**Aire, por favor.**
*ah'ee-ray, pohr fah-vohrr'.*
Let me have some air.

**Necesito un doctor.**
*nay-say-see'toh oon dohk-tohr'.*
I need a doctor.

**Tengo calentura.**
*tayn'goh kah-layn-too'rah.*
I have a fever.

**Tengo un fuerte catarro.**
*tayn'goh oon foo-ayr'tay kah-tah'roh.*
I have a bad cold.

**Me corté.**
*may kohr-tay'.*
I cut myself.

**¿Dónde está la farmacia más cercana?**
*dohn'day ays-tah' lah fahr-mah'see-ah mahs sayr-kah'nah?*
Where is the nearest drugstore?

**Por favor prepáreme esta receta.**
*pohr fah-vohrr' pray-pah'ray-may ays'tah ray-say'tah.*
Please make up this prescription.

**Aspirina.**
*ahs-pee-ree'nah.*
Aspirin.

**Bandaid.**
*bahnd-ah'eed.*
Bandaid.

**Loción para broncear.**
*loh-see-ohn' pah'rah brohn-say-ahr'.*
Suntan lotion.

**Yodo.**
*yoh'doh.*
Iodine.

**Bromo Seltzer.**
*broh'moh sayl'sayr.*
Bromo Seltzer.

**Acido bórico.**
*ah'see-doh boh'ree-koh.*
Boric acid.

**Algodón absorbente.**
*ahl-goh-dohn' ahb-sohr-bayn'tay.*
Absorbent cotton.

**Pomada de óxido de zinc.**
*poh-mah'dah day ohk'see-doh day seenk.*
Zinc salve.

**Loción contra insectos.**
*loh-see-ohn' kohn'trah een-sayk'tohs.*
Insect repellent.

**Loción contra quemaduras de sol.**
*loh-see-ohn' kohn'trah kay-mah-doo'rahs day sohl.*
Sunburn lotion.

# SPORTS

## Golf

**Deseo alquilar unos palos de golf, por favor.**
*day-say'oh ahl-kee-lahr' oo'nohs pah'lohs day gohlf, pohr fah-vohrr'.*
I would like to rent a set of golf clubs, please.

**¿Quiere contratar a un caddy?**
*kee-ay'ray kohn-trah-tahr' ah oon kah'dee?*
Will you want to hire a caddy?

**¿Dónde está la plataforma de salida?**
*dohn'day ays-tah' lah plah-tah-fohr'mah day sah-lee'dah?*
Where do I tee off?

**Caddy, mi palo número uno.**
*kah'dee, mee pah'loh noo'may-roh oo'noh.*
Caddy, my driver, please.

## Swimming

**Deseo alquilar una sombrilla de playa.**
*day-say'oh ahl-kee-lahr' oo'nah sohm-bree'yah day plah'yah.*
I would like to rent a beach umbrella.

**¿Dónde podemos ponernos nuestro traje de baño?**
*dohn'day poh-day'mohs poh-nayr'nohs nways'troh trah'hay day bahn'yoh?*
Where can we change into our bathing suits?

**¿Dónde puedo comprar una loción para el sol?**
*dohn'day pway'doh kohm-prahr' oo'nah loh-see'ohn' pah'rah ayl sohl?*
Where can I buy some suntan lotion?

**Calienta mucho el sol hoy.**
*kah-lee-ayn'tah moo'choh ayl sohl oh'ee.*
The sun is awfully strong, today.

## Fishing and Hunting

**Necesito una caña y carrete, cordel y anzuelos.**
*nay-say-see'toh oo'nah kah'nya ee kah-ray'tay, kohr-dayl' ee ahn-soo ay'lohs.*
I need a rod and reel, some line, and hooks.

**¿Dónde podemos alquilar un bote (lancha)?**
*dohn'day poh-day'mohs ahl-kee-lahr' oon boh'tay (lahn'chah)?*
Where can we rent a boat?

**¿Dónde podemos pescar barracuda?**
*dohn'day poh-day mohs pays--cahr' bah-rah-koo'dah?*
Where can we fish for barracuda?

**¿Dónde puedo comprar cartuchos?**
*dohn'day pway'doh kohm-prahr' kahr-too'chohs?*
Where can I buy ammunition?

**La estación para perdices es de diciembre a marzo.**
*lah ays-tah-see-ohn' pah-rah payr-dee'says ays day dee-see-aym'bray ah mahr'soh.*
The partridge season is from December to March.

## CONDUCTING BUSINESS

**Represento a una compañía americana.**
*ray-pray-sayn'toh ah oo'nah kohm-pah-nyee'ah ah-may-ree-kah'nah.*
I represent an American firm.

**Soy agente viajero.**
*soh'ee ah-hayn'tay vee-ah-hay'roh.*
I am a traveling salesman.

**Estoy aquí para conocer el mercado.**
*ays-toy' ah-kee' pah'rah koh-noh-sayr' ayl mayr-kah'doh.*
I am here to survey the market.

**Necesito un distribuidor local para mi producto.**
*nay-say-see'toh oon dees-tree-bwee-dohr' loh-kahl' pah-rah mee proh-dook'toh.*
I need a local distributor for my product.

**¿Se puede manufacturar este producto aquí?**
*say pway'day mah-noo-fahk-too-rahr' ays'tay proh-dook'toh ah-kee'?*
Can this product be manufactured here?

# OUTLINE OF SPANISH GRAMMAR

Although, for purposes of everyday practical needs, you will be able to get by with some stock of common Spanish words and phrases, it is advisable also to have some understanding of the parts of speech and their various forms as well as of the manner in which Spanish sentences are constructed. In the following pages we have attempted to present the "highlights" of Spanish grammar very concisely, so as to enable you to understand the how and why of the phrases in this book. This survey is of necessity brief, but the main facts for your daily needs have been covered.

## 1. THE ARTICLE

**1.1.** The definite article in Spanish has the following forms:

| | Singular | Plural |
|---|---|---|
| Masculine | **el** (the) | **los** (the) |
| Feminine | **la** (the) | **las** (the) |

**1.2.** Contractions of the masculine singular definite article are formed with the prepositions *a* and *de* : *al* (*a* + *el*) *hombre* (to the man) *del* (*de* + *el*) *hombre* (of the man).

**1.3.** The definite article in Spanish is used more often than in English.

**1.4.** The forms of the indefinite article in Spanish are:

| | Singular | Plural |
|---|---|---|
| Masculine | **un** (a or an) | **unos** (some) |
| Feminine | **una** (a or an) | **unas** (some) |

**1.5.** The indefinite article is not used in Spanish so often as in English.

**1.6.** Both the definite and indefinite articles agree in gender and number with the noun they modify.

**1.7.** The neuter article *lo* is used with participles and adjectives, as *lo dicho* (what has been said), *lo útil* (that which is useful).

## 2. THE NOUN

**2.1.** All nouns in Spanish are either masculine or feminine. Nouns ending in *-o* are generally masculine; those ending in *-a* (except *-ma*

and -*ta*), -*dad*, -*tad*, -*tud*, -*ión*, *umbre*, -*ez*, and *ie* are generally feminine.

**2.2.** The plural of nouns of both genders ending in an unstressed vowel is formed by adding -*s* and of nouns ending in a consonant or a stressed vowel by adding -*es*: *el caballo* (the horse), *los caballos* (the horses); *la yegua* (the mare), *las yeguas* (the mares); *la flor* (the flower), *las flores* (the flowers); *el rubí* (the ruby), *los rubíes* (the rubies).

**2.3.** In Spanish, possession is always expressed by the preposition *de* preceding the noun which designates the possessor: *el libro de Jorge* (George's book).

**2.4.** If the object (direct or indirect) denotes a person, it is preceded by the preposition *a*, which is then called **the personal a**. Compare the following examples: *Espero a mi tía* (I wait for my aunt); *Busco mi abrigo* (I am looking for my overcoat). This personal *a* is omitted when the object denoting a person is not identified: *Llame un policía* (Call a [= any] policeman).

**2.5.** Spanish speakers use a great number of diminutives (which express smallness or affection) and augmentatives (which usually express large size or awkwardness), especially in colloquial speech. These diminutives and augmentatives make the speech more colorful and add various connotations to the basic meanings of the words from which they are derived. One whose native tongue is not Spanish has to be careful in the use of these forms because he may use a diminutive or augmentative formed with a certain suffix which has a basic connotation but which in certain forms may have additional connotations. Examples: *pan* (bread), *panecito* (roll); *Ana* (Anna), *Anita* (Anny); *mano* (hand), *manecita* (pretty little hand); *pueblo* (town), *pueblecillo* (tiny town); *libro* (book), *librito* (booklet), *librote* (large old book); *hombre* (man), *hombrón* (big man).

# 3. THE ADJECTIVE

**3.1.** There are two classes of adjectives in Spanish:

*a*) Those which end in -*o* in the m(asculine) s(ingular) and have four forms (one for the m. s. in -*o*, one for the f(eminine) s. in -*a*, one for the m. pl(ural) in -*os*, and one for the f. pl. in -*as*): *el cuarto pequeño* (the small room), *los cuartos pequeños* (the small rooms); *la casa pequeña* (the small house), *las casas pequeñas* (the small houses).

*b*) Those which end in -*e* or any vowel other than -*o* or in a consonant have only two forms, one for the singular and one for the plural of both genders: *el cuarto grande* (the large room), *la casa grande* (the large house); *los cuartos grandes* (the large rooms), *las casas grandes* (the large rooms).

**3.2.** The adjective agrees in gender and number with the noun it modifies. An adjective which modifies two or more nouns is always used in its masculine plural form if at least one noun is masculine: *Pepe y María son ricos* (Joe and Mary are wealthy).

**3.3.** The adjectives follow the same rules as the nouns for the formation of the plural.

**3.4** In Spanish the usual position of the descriptive adjectives is after the noun they modify: *camino estrecho* (narrow road).

Limiting adjectives, such as demonstrative, interrogative, possessive and indefinite pronominal adjectives and numerals precede the noun they modify: *este libro* (this book); *cualquier libro* (any book [at all]); *el primer libro* (the first book).

Adjectives which express an inherent or characteristic quality of the modified noun or which are used with a figurative meaning also generally precede the noun they modify: *la blanca nieve* (the white snow); *la dura necesidad* (the hard necessity).

Some adjectives change their meaning according to their position before or after the noun, *un gran hombre* (a great man); *un hombre grande* (a big man).

A few adjectives, such as *bueno* (good), *malo* (bad), *pequeño* (small), as well as the ordinal numerals, may appear before or after the noun they modify without any basic change in their meaning.

**3.5.** The adjectives in Spanish, as in English, may be used as nouns: *el español* ([the] Spanish [language]); *los pobres y los ricos* (the poor and the rich).

**3.6.** The comparative is formed by placing *más* (more) before the adjective: *más hermoso* (more beautiful). The superlative is formed by adding the article to the comparative: *el (la) más hermoso(-a)* (the most beautiful).

Four adjectives have irregular comparative forms: *bueno* (good), *mejor* (better); *malo* (bad), *peor* (worse); *grande* (big), *mayor* or *más grande* (larger); *pequeño* (little), *menor* or *más pequeño* (smaller).

The comparison of superiority is expressed by *más* plus the adjective plus *que* and that of inferiority by *menos* plus the adjective plus *que*: *Ella es menos pobre que él* (She is less poor than he).

# 4. THE PRONOUN

**4.1.** The personal pronouns are:

### Singular

|  | Subject | Indirect object | Direct object | Prepositional (used after prepositions) |
|---|---|---|---|---|
| yo | *I* | me | me | mí | *me* |
| tú (fam.) | *you* | te | te | ti | *you* |
| él | *he* | le | le, lo | él | *him* |
| ella | *she* | le | la | ella | *her* |
| usted | *you* | le | le, lo (m.), la (f.) | usted | *you* |
| él, ella | *it* | le | lo (m.), la (f.) | él, ella, ello | *it* |

### Plural

|  | Subject | Indirect object | Direct object | Prepositional |
|---|---|---|---|---|
| nosotros,-as | *we* | nos | nos | nosotros,-as | *us* |
| vosotros,-as (f.) | *you* | os | os | vosotros,-as | *you* |
| ellos | *they* | les | los | ellos | *them* |
| ellas | *they* | les | las | ellas | *them* |
| ustedes | *you* | les | los (m.), las (f.) | ustedes | *you* |

The object pronouns are placed before the verb. Only in the case of an infinitive, an imperative or a gerund, are they placed after the verb and attached to it: *El me la\* pagó* (He paid it to me); *Páguemela\** (Pay it to me).

The indirect object must precede the direct object when a verb governs two object pronouns.

When both the direct and indirect object pronouns are in the third person, *se* is used for the indirect objects *le* and *les*: *Se lo doy* (I give it to him [her, them, you sing. and pl.]).

For emphasis and to avoid ambiguity, the prepositional pronouns are used in addition to the object pronouns: *El se la\* pagó a usted.* (He paid it to you); *Páguesela\** (Pay it to her).

When the pronouns *mí, ti, sí* are governed by the preposition *con* (with), they form one word consisting of *con*, the pronoun and the particle *-go*: *conmigo* (with me), *contigo* (with you), *consigo* (with him, her, it, them).

**4.2. Reflexive pronouns.** The pronouns of the first, second and

---

\* La in all these cases refers to *la cuenta* (bill).

third persons have a reflexive meaning when they refer to the same person as the subject:

| | |
|---|---|
| *(Yo) me equivoco* | I am mistaken |
| *(Tú) te equivocas* | You are mistaken |
| *(El) se equivoca* | He is mistaken |
| *(Nosotros) nos equivocamos* | We are mistaken |
| *(Vosotros) os equivócais* | You are mistaken |
| *(Ellos) se equivocan* | They are mistaken |

*Usted* and *ustedes* (polite forms of you) are also replaced by *se* in the reflexive form: *Se equivoca(n) usted(es)* (you are mistaken).

**4.3. The possessive adjectives** are:

| SHORT FORMS | | LONG FORMS | | *English* |
|---|---|---|---|---|
| *(used before a noun)* | | *(used after a noun)* | | *equivalents* |
| **Singular** | **Plural** | **Singular** | **Plural** | my |
| *mi* | *mis* | *mío, -a* | *míos, -as* | your |
| *tu* | *tus* | *tuyo, -a* | *tuyos, -as* | his, her, its, |
| *su* | *sus* | *suyo, -a* | *suyos, -as* | your, their |
| *nuestro, -a* | *nuestros, -as* | *nuestro, -a* | *nuestros, -as* | our |
| *vuestro, -a* | *vuestros, -as* | *vuestro, -a* | *vuestros, -as* | your |

The forms of the possessive pronouns in Spanish are identical with the long forms of the possessive adjectives, but they are preceded by the definite article: *el mío* (m. s.); *los míos* (m. pl.); *la mía* (f. s.); *las mías* (f. pl.) (mine). They agree in gender and number with the noun for which they stand.

The relative possessive adjective is *cuyo (-a)* which agrees in gender and number with the noun that follows it: *El viejo cuya casa compré está aquí* (The old man whose house I bought is here).

**4.4. The interrogative pronouns** are:

*¿Quién?* (who? whom), of both genders, refers to persons only.

*¿Qué?* (what)) , used with things and in many other cases.

*¿Cuál?* (which, which one?), used to select one from a large group of persons or things.

Only *quién* and *cuál* have plural forms. They are *quiénes* and *cuáles*.

**4.5. The demonstrative pronouns and adjectives.** There is no difference in form between the demonstrative pronouns *éste, ésta* (this one); *éstos, éstas* (these ones); *ése, ésa* (that one); *ésos, ésas* (those ones); *aquél, aquélla* (that one) ; and *aquéllos, aquéllas* (those ones) and the corresponding demonstrative adjectives *este, esta* (this); *estos, estas* (these); *esos, esas* (those); *aquel, aquella* (that); and *aquellos, aquellas* (those). The only difference between the two groups is that the pronouns have a written accent on the stressed syllable while the adjectives are written without any accent. The demonstrative pronouns stand by themselves, but the demonstrative adjectives precede the nouns which they limit and modify. Examples: Adjective: *Este baúl es de Ricardo* (This trunk is Richard's). Pronoun: *Este es mi baúl* (This is my trunk).

The *este*-forms indicate an object which is near the person who speaks; the *ese*-forms an object near the person addressed; and the *aquel*-forms an object which is removed from both the speaker and the person addressed.

In addition to the demonstrative pronouns, which have corresponding forms used as demonstrative adjectives, there are the neuter pronouns *esto, eso,* and *aquello* which have no written accent and are used when the thing for which they stand is a statement, idea or something indefinite or unknown: *Esto es muy bueno* (This is very good); *¡Eso es!* (That's it!).

**4.6.a.** The most common **indefinite pronouns** in Spanish are:

*Alguien* (someone, somebody, anyone, anybody), which refers to persons only.

*Algun(o), -a, -os, -as* (someone, -body; anyone, -body) which refers to persons or things.

*Cualquiera* (any one), which refers to persons only.

*Nadie* (no one, nobody, none, no), which refers to persons only.

*Ningun(o), -a, -os, -as* (no one, nobody, none, no), which refers to persons or things.

*Otro, -a* (another, other), *otros, -as* (others), which refer to persons or things.

**4.6.b.** The most common **indefinite adjectives** in Spanish are:

1. Those that have four forms:

| | |
|---|---|
| *alguno, -a, -os, -as* | some, any, a few |
| *(alguno, -a que otro, -a* | some . . . or other) |
| *mucho, -a, -os, -as* | much, many |
| *ninguno -a, (-os, -as)* | not any, no |
| *otro, -a, -os, -as* | another, other |
| *poco, -a, -os, -as* | little, few |
| *tanto, -a, -os, -as* | as much, as many |
| *todo, -a, -os, -as* | all, every |

2. Those that have only one form: *cada* (each), *los (las) demás* (the rest [of]).

3. Those that have two forms: *ambos, ambas* (both), *cualquiera, cualesquiera* (any [one] at all).

**4.7. Relative pronouns.** *Que* (who, whom, that, which) is the most common of the relative pronouns. It is used either as a subject or the direct object of a verb: *El libro que me dió usted es muy interesante* (The book [which] you gave me is very interesting); *Me gusta el libro que me dió usted* (I like the book [which] you gave me). Note in the above sentence that the word "which" or "that" (*que*), which may be and is often omitted in English, can *never* be omitted in Spanish.

*Quien* (who, whom) is used instead of *que* after prepositions and to introduce clauses which are not necessary to complete a sentence: *El niño de quien hablé está aqui* (The child of whom I spoke is here).

*El que, la que, los que, las que; el cual, la cual, los cuales, las cuales* may be used instead of *que* or *quien* to avoid ambiguity: *El perro de mi amiga, el cual desaparece a menudo, no está aquí ahora* (My girl friend's dog, which disappears often, is not here now).

*Lo que* (that which, what, which) is used as a relative pronoun which refers to a fact, an event, or an idea rather than to a person or a thing.

# 5. THE NUMERALS

**5.1.** The cardinal numbers are listed on page 20. They are all invariable, except *uno (-a)* and the compounds of *ciento* (a hundred), as *doscientos, -as* (two hundred), etc.

*Uno* drops the *-o* and *ciento* its final syllable *-to* when they immediately precede a noun.

**5.2.** The ordinal numbers are inflected exactly as adjectives. *Primero* and *tercero* drop the final *-o* when they precede a noun: *el tercer tomo* (the third volume).

# 6. THE PREPOSITION

**6.1.** The use of the prepositions is one of the most difficult things to master in learning a foreign language because prepositional usage is largely idiomatic. You should form the habit of observing and learning, through repetition and practice, the prepositional usages which differ from English as you encounter them.

The most common prepositions in Spanish are: *a* (to [direction]), *ante, antes de* (before [time]), *bajo* (under), *con* (with), *contra* (against), *de* (from), *delante de* (before [place]), *desde* (since), *después de* (after) [time]), *detrás de* (behind [place]), *durante* (during), *en* (in, on), *entre* (between), *hacia* (toward [direction]), *hasta* (until), *para* (for [purpose, aim]), *por* (through, for [means, reason]), *según* (according to), *sin* (without), *sobre* (on, over), *tras* (after).

# 7. THE ADVERB

**7.1.** In Spanish, most of the adverbs of manner are formed by adding the suffix *-mente* to the singular feminine forms of adjectives:

| | | | |
|---|---|---|---|
| *rápido, -a* | quick | *rápidamente* | quickly |
| *fácil* | easy | *fácilmente* | easily |

**7.2.** In a series of adverbs in *-mente,* the suffix *-mente* is omitted from all except the last.

**7.3.** The comparative of adverbs is formed by placing *más* before the adverb; and the superlative by placing *lo más* before it.

Four very common adverbs have irregular comparatives: *bien* (well), *mejor* (better); *mal* (badly), *peor* (worse); *mucho* (much), *más* (more); *poco* (little), *menos* (less).

**7.4.** *Donde* is used as both interrogative and affirmative "where". In writing, the interrogative *dónde* takes an accent.

# 8. THE CONJUNCTION

**8.1.** Coordinating conjunctions join sentences, clauses, phrases, and words of equal rank. The most common ones in Spanish are: *y* (and), *o* (or), *pero, mas* (but); and the correlatives: *o . . . o* (either . . . or), *ni . . . ni* (neither . . . nor).

When *y* occurs before a word beginning with *i* or *hi,* it changes to *e,* and *o* before *o* or *ho* changes to *u.*

**8.2.** Subordinating conjunctions introduce dependent clauses. The most common ones are: *a fin de que* (in order to), *aunque* (although), *como* (as), *conque* (so that, so then), *con tal que* (provided that), *cuando* (when), *mientras que* (while), *para (que)* (in order to), *porque* (because), *puesto que* (since), *que* (that), *si* (if).

# 9. THE INTERJECTION

**9.1.** Some of the most common interjections in Spanish, and their approximate English meanings, are: *¡ay!* (ouch!, ah!, alas!), *¡ah!* (ah!), *¡bah!* (pshaw!), *¡hola!* (hello!), *¡viva!* (hurrah!), *¡caramba!* (confound it!).

**9.2.** Exclamative phrases are used as interjections:

| | |
|---|---|
| *¡Qué bonita!* (How pretty!) | *¡Qué lástima!* (What a pity!) |
| *¡Qué hermosa!* (How beautiful!) | *¡No importa!* (Never mind!) |

# 10. THE VERB

**10.1.** In English the form of the verb changes according to the subject. We say: I am, you are, he is, etc. In most cases, however, the English verb changes only in the third person singular in the present. Since most of the possible forms are identical, we are not especially conscious of the problem of verb endings. On the other hand, the Spanish verb has a large number of endings which differ according to subject, tense, and mood. The best way to learn the verb forms properly is in the context in which they are used.

There are three conjugations in Spanish and they are indicated by the ending of the infinitive:

| 1ST CONJUGATION | 2ND CONJUGATION | 3RD CONJUGATION |
|---|---|---|
| **dese-ar** | **com-er** | **part-ir** |
| (to wish) | (to eat) | (to leave; to divide) |

The stem of a verb is what is left after striking off the ending of the infinitive. The endings of the different moods, tenses, and persons are added to these stems.

## 10.2 INDICATIVE

### Present

The Spanish *deseo* corresponds to the English "I wish," "I am wishing," "I do wish."

| | First Conjugation | Second Conjugation | Third Conjugation |
|---|---|---|---|
| yo | dese-*o* | com-*o* | part-*o* |
| | (*I wish*) | (*I eat*) | (*I leave*) |
| tú | dese-*as* | com-*es* | part-*es* |
| usted (él, ella) | dese-*a* | com-*e* | part-*e* |
| nos | dese-*amos* | com-*emos* | part-*imos* |
| vos | dese-*áis* | com-*éis* | part-*ís* |
| ustedes ellos, ellas | dese-*an* | com-*en* | part-*en* |

The pronouns (*yo*, etc.) may be omitted in Spanish because the endings themselves indicate the subject (see **4.1**).

The present indicative of regular verbs is formed by taking the stem of the verb and adding to it the endings which are printed in italics to help the student distinguish them.

### Imperfect

*(I wished, was wishing, used to wish, eat, leave, etc.)*

| | | |
|---|---|---|
| dese-*aba* | com-*ía* | part-*ía* |
| dese-*abas* | com-*ías* | part-*ías* |
| dese-*aba* | com-*ía* | part-*ía* |
| dese-*ábamos* | com-*íamos* | part-*íamos* |
| dese-*abais* | com-*íais* | part-*íais* |
| dese-*aban* | com-*ían* | part-*ían* |

Note that the second and third conjugations have identical endings for the imperfect.

### Future

*(I shall or will wish, eat, leave, etc.)*

| | | |
|---|---|---|
| dese-*aré* | com-*eré* | part-*iré* |
| dese-*arás* | com-*erás* | part-*irás* |
| dese-*ará* | com-*erá* | part-*irá* |
| dese-*aremos* | com-*eremos* | part-*iremos* |
| dese-*aréis* | com-*eréis* | part-*iréis* |
| dese-*arán* | com-*erán* | part-*irán* |

### Preterit

| | | |
|---|---|---|
| dese-*é* | com-*í* | part-*í* |
| *(I wished)* | *(I ate)* | *(I left)* |
| dese-*aste* | com-*iste* | part-*iste* |
| dese-*ó* | com-*ió* | part-*ió* |
| dese-*amos* | com-*imos* | part-*imos* |
| dese-*asteis* | com-*isteis* | part-*isteis* |
| dese-*aron* | com-*ieron* | part-*ieron* |

### Conditional

*(I should or would wish, eat, leave, etc.)*

| | | |
|---|---|---|
| dese-*aría* | com-*ería* | part-*iría* |
| dese-*arías* | com-*erías* | part-*irías* |
| dese-*aría* | com-*ería* | part-*iría* |
| dese-*aríamos* | com-*eríamos* | part-*iríamos* |
| dese-*aríais* | com-*eríais* | part-*iríais* |
| dese-*arían* | com-*erían* | part-*irían* |

## COMPOUND TENSES

All compound tenses of both the indicative and the subjunctive are formed by the proper tense of the auxiliary verb *haber* plus the past participle.

### Perfect

(Formed by the present of *haber* plus the past participle.)

| | | | | | |
|---|---|---|---|---|---|
| he | dese-*ado* | he | com-*ido* | he | part-*ido* |
| has | dese-*ado* | has | com-*ido* | has | part-*ido* |
| ha | dese-*ado* | ha | com-*ido* | ha | part-*ido* |
| hemos | dese-*ado* | hemos | com-*ido* | hemos | part-*ido* |
| habéis | dese-*ado* | habéis | com-*ido* | habéis | part-*ido* |
| han | dese-*ado* | han | com-*ido* | han | part-*ido* |

### Pluperfect

(Formed by the imperfect of *haber* plus the past participle.)

| | | | | | |
|---|---|---|---|---|---|
| había | deseado | había | comido | había | partido |
| habías | deseado | habías | comido | habías | partido |
| había | deseado | había | comido | había | partido |
| habíamos | deseado | habíamos | comido | habíamos | partido |
| habías | deseado | habíais | comido | habías | partido |
| habían | deseado | habían | comido | habían | partido |

#### FUTURE PERFECT AND CONDITIONAL PERFECT

The future perfect is formed by the future of *haber* and the past participle of the verb, and the conditional perfect by the conditional of *haber* and the past participle.

| **Future Perfect** | | **Conditional Perfect** | |
|---|---|---|---|
| *(I shall have wished, eaten, left, etc.)* | | *(I should have wished, eaten, left, etc.)* | |
| habré | | habría | |
| habrás | | habrías | |
| habrá | dese-ado | habría | dese-ado |
| habremos | com-ido | habríamos | com-ido |
| habréis | part-ido | habríais | part-ido |
| habrán | | habrían | |

## 10.3 THE SUBJUNCTIVE

The subjunctive in Spanish is used in subordinate clauses in which action is presented as a possibility and not as a fact, and after imper-

The subjunctive in Spanish is used in dependent clauses in which action is presented as a possibility and not a a fact, and after impersonal expressions introduced by *que* (that). Examples: *Creo que él lo haga* (I think that he may (will) do it); *Esperan que ella vuelva mañana* (They hope that she may (will) return tomorrow); *Es necesario que yo salga en seguida* (It is necessary for me to leave at once).

Note that in the first example the present subjunctive is used for both present and future time. The word "que" must never be omitted even when its corresponding word "that" in English is omitted.

When *creer* and other verbs of similar meaning in the main clause express certainty, the indicative is used in the dependent clause; when they express doubt or possibility, the subjunctive is used. Examples: *Creo que ellos son buenos* (I believe they are good); *Creo que ellos sean buenos* (I think that they may (will) be good).

When the verb of the main clause expresses desire, command, fear, wonder and similar emotions, the subjunctive is used in the dependent clause. Examples: *Ella quiere que usted compre eso* (She wants you to buy that); *Yo no quiero hacerlo pero él quiere que yo lo haga* (I don't want to do it, but he wants me to do it).

Note that when the subject is the same for both the main and the dependent verbs, the infinitive is used, as in English, but when the subject is different, the subjunctive is used in a dependent clause.

The tenses of the subjunctive are the present, the imperfect, the perfect and the pluperfect.

### Present Subjunctive

| | | |
|---|---|---|
| dese-*e* | com-*a* | part-*a* |
| dese-*es* | com-*as* | part-*as* |
| dese-*e* | com-*a* | part-*a* |
| dese-*emos* | com-*amos* | part-*amos* |
| dese-*éis* | com-*áis* | part-*áis* |
| dese-*en* | com-*an* | part-*an* |

### Imperfect Subjunctive

The imperfect subjunctive has two forms, the "*ra*" form and the "*se*" form. The two forms have the same meaning. They may be used indiscriminately.

### The Ra-Subjunctive

| | | |
|---|---|---|
| dese-*ara* | com-*iera* | part-*iera* |
| dese-*aras* | com-*ieras* | part-*ieras* |
| dese-*ara* | com-*iera* | part-*iera* |
| dese-*áramos* | com-*iéramos* | part-*iéramos* |
| dese-*arais* | com-*ierais* | part-*ierais* |
| dese-*aran* | com-*ieran* | part-*ieran* |

### The Se-Subjunctive

| | | |
|---|---|---|
| dese-*ase* | com-*iese* | part-*iese* |
| dese-*ases* | com-*ieses* | part-*ieses* |
| dese-*ase* | com-*iese* | part-*iese* |
| dese-*ásemos* | com-*iésemos* | part-*iésemos* |
| dese-*aseis* | com-*ieseis* | part-*ieseis* |
| dese-*asen* | com-*iesen* | part-*iesen* |

The perfect and pluperfect subjunctives are formed by the present and imperfect subjunctives, respectively, of *haber* plus the past participle of the verb.

## 10.4 THE IMPERATIVE

The true imperative is used only in the familiar form of affirmative commands: *come* (eat [singular]), *comed* (eat [plural; very seldom used]).

The third person of the present subjunctive is used for the polite imperative: *coma* (eat). This is the form of the imperative used under normal circumstances and corresponds to the *usted*-form of the indicative and the subjunctive.

## 10.5 THE PARTICIPLES

The gerund or present participle is invariable in gender and number. It is used most frequently in connection with the verb *estar* to form the progressive tenses, and it expresses an action that continues or is continued:

| **Estoy hablando** | **Estaremos comiendo** | **¿Está lloviendo?** |
|---|---|---|
| I am speaking | We shall be eating | Is it raining? |

The past participle is formed by adding -*ado* to the stem of the verbs of the first conjugation and -*ido* to those of the second and third conjugations:

**dese-ado** (wished)   **com-ido** (eaten)   **part-ido** (left)

There is a small number of verbs which have irregular past participles.

**10.6.** The two Spanish verbs *ser* and *estar* corresponding to the English "to be" are included among the irregular verbs of the list. *Ser* is used with predicate adjectives to denote an inherent quality. *Estar* is used to denote a temporary quality or position.

**10.7.** The following pages list the most common irregular verbs in Spanish in the basic tenses and moods. The forms printed in bold face are irregular, and those in light face are regular.

# IRREGULAR

| INFINITIVE & PARTICIPLES | INDICATIVE | | | |
|---|---|---|---|---|
| | PRESENT | IMPERFECT | PRETERIT | FUTURE |
| **andar,** *to walk* andando andado | ando andas anda andamos andáis andan | andaba andabas andaba andábamos andabais andaban | **anduve** **anduviste** **anduvo** **anduvimos** **anduvisteis** **anduvieron** | andaré andarás andará andaremos andaréis andarán |
| **caber,** *to fit into* cabiendo cabido | **quepo** cabes cabe cabemos cabéis caben | cabía cabías cabía cabíamos cabíais cabían | **cupe** **cupiste** **cupo** **cupimos** **cupisteis** **cupieron** | **cabré** **cabrás** **cabrá** **cabremos** **cabréis** **cabrán** |
| **caer,** *to fall* **cayendo** **caído** | **caigo** caes cae caemos caéis caen | caía caías caía caíamos caíais caían | **caí** **caíste** **cayó** **caímos** **caísteis** **cayeron** | caeré caerás caerá caeremos caeréis caerán |
| **dar,** *to give* dando dado | **doy** das da damos dais dan ⸍ | daba dabas daba dábamos dabais daban | **di** **diste** **dió** **dimos** **disteis** **dieron** | daré darás dará daremos daréis darán |
| **decir,** *to say, tell* **diciendo** **dicho** | **digo** **dices** **dice** **decimos** **decís** **dicen** | decía decías decía decíamos decíais decían | **dije** **dijiste** **dijo** **dijimos** **dijisteis** **dijeron** | **diré** **dirás** **dirá** **diremos** **diréis** **dirán** |
| **estar,** *to be* estando estado | **estoy** **estás** **está** **estamos** **estáis** **están** | estaba estabas estaba estábamos estabais estaban | **estuve** **estuviste** **estuvo** **estuvimos** **estuvisteis** **estuvieron** | estaré estarás estará estaremos estaréis estarán |
| **haber,** *to have* habiendo habido | **he** **has** **ha** **hemos** **habéis** **han** | había habías había habíamos habíais habían | **hube** **hubiste** **hubo** **hubimos** **hubisteis** **hubieron** | **habré** **habrás** **habrá** **habremos** **habréis** **habrán** |

# VERBS

| CONDITIONAL | IMPERATIVE | SUBJUNCTIVE | | |
| --- | --- | --- | --- | --- |
| | | PRESENT | IMPERFECT 1 | IMPERFECT 2 |
| andaría | anda | ande | anduviese | anduviera |
| andarías | andad | andes | anduvieses | anduvieras |
| andaría | | ande | anduviese | anduviera |
| andaríamos | | andemos | anduviésemos | anduviéramos |
| andaríais | | andéis | anduvieseis | anduvierais |
| andarían | | anden | anduviesen | anduvieran |
| **cabría** | cabe | **quepa** | cupiese | cupiera |
| **cabrías** | cabed | **quepas** | cupieses | cupieras |
| **cabría** | | **quepa** | cupiese | cupiera |
| **cabríamos** | | **quepamos** | cupiésemos | cupiéramos |
| **cabríais** | | **quepáis** | cupieseis | cupierais |
| **cabrían** | | **quepan** | cupiesen | cupieran |
| caería | cae | caiga | cayese | cayera |
| caerías | caed | caigas | cayeses | cayeras |
| caería | | caiga | cayese | cayera |
| caeríamos | | caigamos | cayésemos | cayéramos |
| caeríais | | caigáis | cayeseis | cayerais |
| caerían | | caigan | cayesen | cayeran |
| daría | da | dé | diese | diera |
| darías | dad | des | dieses | dieras |
| daría | | dé | diese | diera |
| daríamos | | demos | diésemos | diéramos |
| daríais | | deis | dieseis | dierais |
| darían | | den | diesen | dieran |
| diría | di | diga | dijese | dijera |
| dirías | decid | digas | dijeses | dijeras |
| diría | | diga | dijese | dijera |
| diríamos | | digamos | dijésemos | dijéramos |
| diríais | | digáis | dijeseis | dijerais |
| dirían | | digan | dijesen | dijeran |
| estaría | **está** | esté | estuviese | estuviera |
| estarías | estad | estés | estuvieses | estuvieras |
| estaría | | esté | estuviese | estuviera |
| estaríamos | | estemos | estuviésemos | estuviéramos |
| estaríais | | estéis | estuvieseis | estuvierais |
| estarían | | estén | estuviesen | estuvieran |
| **habría** | he | haya | hubiese | hubiera |
| **habrías** | habed | hayas | hubieses | hubieras |
| **habría** | | haya | hubiese | hubiera |
| **habríamos** | | hayamos | hubiésemos | hubiéramos |
| **habríais** | | hayáis | hubieseis | hubierais |
| **habrían** | | hayan | hubiesen | hubieran |

| INFINITIVE & PARTICIPLES | INDICATIVE | | | |
|---|---|---|---|---|
| | PRESENT | IMPERFECT | PRETERIT | FUTURE |
| hacer, *to make, do* haciendo hecho | hago haces hace hacemos hacéis hacen | hacía hacías hacía hacíamos hacíais hacían | hice hiciste hizo hicimos hicisteis hicieron | haré harás hará haremos haréis harán |
| ir, *to go* yendo ido | voy vas va vamos vais van | iba ibas iba íbamos ibais iban | fui fuiste fue fuimos fuisteis fueron | iré irás irá iremos iréis irán |
| oír, *to hear* oyendo oído | oigo oyes oye oímos oís oyen | oía oías oía oíamos oíais oían | oí oíste oyó oímos oísteis oyeron | oiré oirás oirá oiremos oiréis oirán |
| poder, *to be able* pudiendo podido | puedo puedes puede podemos podéis pueden | podía podías podía podíamos podíais podían | pude pudiste pudo pudimos pudisteis pudieron | podré podrás podrá podremos podréis podrán |
| poner, *to put* poniendo puesto | pongo pones pone ponemos ponéis ponen | ponía ponías ponía poníamos poníais ponían | puse pusiste puso pusimos pusisteis pusieron | pondré pondrás pondrá pondremos pondréis pondrán |
| querer, *to want* queriendo querido | quiero quieres quiere queremos queréis quieren | quería querías quería queríamos queríais querían | quise quisiste quiso quisimos quisisteis quisieron | querré querrás querrá querremos querréis querrán |
| saber, *to know* sabiendo sabido | sé sabes sabe sabemos sabéis saben | sabía sabías sabía sabíamos sabíais sabían | supe supiste supo supimos supisteis supieron | sabré sabrás sabrá sabremos sabréis sabrán |

| CONDITIONAL | IMPERATIVE | SUBJUNCTIVE | | |
| --- | --- | --- | --- | --- |
| | | PRESENT | IMPERFECT 1 | IMPERFECT 2 |
| haría | haz | haga | hiciese | hiciera |
| harías | haced | hagas | hicieses | hicieras |
| haría | | haga | hiciese | hiciera |
| haríamos | | hagamos | hiciésemos | hiciéramos |
| haríais | | hagáis | hicieseis | hicierais |
| harían | | hagan | hiciesen | hicieran |
| iría | ve | vaya | fuese | fuera |
| irías | id | vayas | fueses | fueras |
| iría | | vaya | fuese | fuera |
| iríamos | | vayamos | fuésemos | fuéramos |
| iríais | | vayáis | fueseis | fuerais |
| irían | | vayan | fuesen | fueran |
| oiría | oye | oiga | oyese | oyera |
| oirías | oíd | oigas | oyeses | oyeras |
| oiría | | oiga | oyese | oyera |
| oiríamos | | oigamos | oyésemos | oyéramos |
| oiríais | | oigáis | oyeseis | oyerais |
| oirían | | oigan | oyesen | oyeran |
| podría | | pueda | pudiese | pudiera |
| podrías | | puedas | pudieses | pudieras |
| podría | | pueda | pudiese | pudiera |
| podríamos | | podamos | pudiésemos | pudiéramos |
| podríais | | podáis | pudieseis | pudierais |
| podrían | | puedan | pudiesen | pudieran |
| pondría | pon | ponga | pusiese | pusiera |
| pondrías | poned | pongas | pusieses | pusieras |
| pondría | | ponga | pusiese | pusiera |
| pondríamos | | pongamos | pusiésemos | pusiéramos |
| pondríais | | pongáis | pusieseis | pusierais |
| pondrían | | pongan | pusiesen | pusieran |
| querría | quiere | quiera | quisiese | quisiera |
| querrías | quered | quieras | quisieses | quisieras |
| querría | | quiera | quisiese | quisiera |
| querríamos | | queramos | quisiésemos | quisiéramos |
| querríais | | queráis | quisieseis | quisierais |
| querrían | | quieran | quisiesen | quisieran |
| sabría | sabe | sepa | supiese | supiera |
| sabrías | sabed | sepas | supieses | supieras |
| sabría | | sepa | supiese | supiera |
| sabríamos | | sepamos | supiésemos | supiéramos |
| sabríais | | sepáis | supieseis | supierais |
| sabrían | | sepan | supiesen | supieran |

| INFINITIVE & PARTICIPLES | INDICATIVE | | | |
|---|---|---|---|---|
| | PRESENT | IMPERFECT | PRETERIT | FUTURE |
| **salir,** | **salgo** | salía | salí | **saldré** |
| *to go out* | **sales** | salías | saliste | **saldrás** |
| saliendo | **sale** | salía | salió | **saldrá** |
| salido | **salimos** | salíamos | salimos | **saldremos** |
| | **salís** | salíais | salisteis | **saldréis** |
| | **salen** | salían | salieron | **saldrán** |
| **ser,** *to be* | **soy** | **era** | **fui** | seré |
| **siendo** | **eres** | **eras** | **fuiste** | serás |
| **sido** | **es** | **era** | **fue** | será |
| | **somos** | **éramos** | **fuimos** | seremos |
| | **sois** | **erais** | **fuisteis** | seréis |
| | **son** | **eran** | **fueron** | serán |
| **tener,** | **tengo** | tenía | **tuve** | **tendré** |
| *to have* | **tienes** | tenías | **tuviste** | **tendrás** |
| teniendo | **tiene** | tenía | **tuvo** | **tendrá** |
| tenido | **tenemos** | teníamos | **tuvimos** | **tendremos** |
| | **tenéis** | teníais | **tuvisteis** | **tendréis** |
| | **tienen** | tenían | **tuvieron** | **tendrán** |
| **traducir,** | **traduzco** | traducía | **traduje** | traduciré |
| *to translate* | **traduces** | traducías | **tradujiste** | traducirás |
| traduciendo | **traduce** | traducía | **tradujo** | traducirá |
| traducido | **traducimos** | traducíamos | **tradujimos** | traduciremos |
| | **traducís** | traducíais | **tradujisteis** | traduciréis |
| | **traducen** | traducían | **tradujeron** | traducirán |
| **traer,** | **traigo** | traía | **traje** | traeré |
| *to bring* | **traes** | traías | **trajiste** | traerás |
| **trayendo** | **trae** | traía | **trajo** | traerá |
| **traído** | **traemos** | traíamos | **trajimos** | traeremos |
| | **traéis** | traíais | **trajisteis** | traeréis |
| | **traen** | traían | **trajeron** | traerán |
| **valer,** | **valgo** | valía | valí | **valdré** |
| *to be worth* | **vales** | valías | valiste | **valdrás** |
| valiendo | **vale** | valía | valió | **valdrá** |
| valido | **valemos** | valíamos | valimos | **valdremos** |
| | **valéis** | valíais | valisteis | **valdréis** |
| | **valen** | valían | valieron | **valdrán** |
| **venir,** | **vengo** | venía | **vine** | **vendré** |
| *to come* | **vienes** | venías | **viniste** | **vendrás** |
| **viniendo** | **viene** | venía | **vino** | **vendrá** |
| **venido** | **venimos** | veníamos | **vinimos** | **vendremos** |
| | **venís** | veníais | **vinisteis** | **vendréis** |
| | **vienen** | venían | **vinieron** | **vendrán** |
| **ver,** *to see* | **veo** | **veía** | **ví** | veré |
| **viendo** | **ves** | **veías** | **viste** | verás |
| **visto** | **ve** | **veía** | **vió** | verá |
| | **vemos** | **veíamos** | **vimos** | veremos |
| | **veis** | **veíais** | **visteis** | veréis |
| | **ven** | **veían** | **vieron** | verán |

| CONDITIONAL | IMPERATIVE | SUBJUNCTIVE | | |
| | | PRESENT | IMPERFECT 1 | IMPERFECT 2 |
|---|---|---|---|---|
| saldría | sal | salga | saliese | saliera |
| saldrías | salid | salgas | salieses | salieras |
| saldría | | salga | saliese | saliera |
| saldríamos | | salgamos | saliésemos | saliéramos |
| saldríais | | salgáis | salieseis | salierais |
| saldrían | | salgan | saliesen | salieran |
| sería | sé | sea | fuese | fuera |
| serías | sed | seas | fueses | fueras |
| sería | | sea | fuese | fuera |
| seríamos | | seamos | fuésemos | fuéramos |
| seríais | | seáis | fueseis | fuerais |
| serían | | sean | fuesen | fueran |
| tendría | ten | tenga | tuviese | tuviera |
| tendrías | tened | tengas | tuvieses | tuvieras |
| tendría | | tenga | tuviese | tuviera |
| tendríamos | | tengamos | tuviésemos | tuviéramos |
| tendríais | | tengáis | tuvieseis | tuvierais |
| tendrían | | tengan | tuviesen | tuvieran |
| traduciría | traduce | traduzca | tradujese | tradujera |
| traducirías | traducid | traduzcas | tradujeses | tradujeras |
| traduciría | | traduzca | tradujese | tradujera |
| traduciríamos | | traduzcamos | tradujésemos | tradujéramos |
| traduciríais | | traduzcáis | tradujeseis | tradujerais |
| traducirían | | traduzcan | tradujesen | tradujeran |
| traería | trae | traiga | trajese | trajera |
| traerías | traed | traigas | trajeses | trajeras |
| traería | | traiga | trajese | trajera |
| traeríamos | | traigamos | trajésemos | trajéramos |
| traeríais | | traigáis | trajeseis | trajerais |
| traerían | | traigan | trajesen | trajeran |
| valdría | val(e) | valga | valiese | valiera |
| valdrías | valed | valgas | valieses | valieras |
| valdría | | valga | valiese | valiera |
| valdríamos | | valgamos | valiésemos | valiéramos |
| valdríais | | valgáis | valieseis | valierais |
| valdrían | | valgan | valiesen | valieran |
| vendría | ven | venga | viniese | viniera |
| vendrías | venid | vengas | vinieses | vinieras |
| vendría | | venga | viniese | viniera |
| vendríamos | | vengamos | viniésemos | viniéramos |
| vendríais | | vengáis | vinieseis | vinierais |
| vendrían | | vengan | viniesen | vinieran |
| vería | ve | vea | viese | viera |
| verías | ved | veas | vieses | vieras |
| vería | | vea | viese | viera |
| veríamos | | veamos | viésemos | viéramos |
| veríais | | veáis | vieseis | vierais |
| verían | | vean | viesen | vieran |

# USEFUL INFORMATION FOR MOTORISTS

**NARROW ROAD**

**DETOUR AT M**

**NARROW BRIDGE**

**PAVEMENT ENDS**

**STOP**

**SLOW**

**SHARP TURN**

**R.R. CROSSING**

**CURVE**

**ROAD CROSSING**

**ROAD JUNCTION**

**MEN AT WORK**

ROAD SIGNS

# SPANISH-ENGLISH DICTIONARY

## A

**a** at, to
**abajo** below
**abierto,-a** open
**abogado** *m.* lawyer
**abrigo** *m.* overcoat
**abril** *m.* April
**abrir** to open
**absolutamente** absolutely
**abuela** *f.* grandmother
**abuelo** *m.* grandfather
**acaso** perhaps
**accidental** accidental
**accidente** *m.* accident
**acción** *f.* action
**aceituna** *f.* olive
**acelerador** *m.* accelerator
**acera** *f.* sidewalk
**acerca de** concerning,
  with regard to
**acompañar** to accompany
**acordar** to remind
**acordarse** to remember
**acostar** to lay down,
  to put to bed
**acostarse** to go to bed,
  to lie down
**actor** *m.* actor
**actriz** *f.* actress
**acuático,-a** aquatic
**acumulador** *m.* battery
**adelantado,-a** advanced, fast
**adelante** forward
**adentro** inside
**admirable** wonderful,
  admirable
**adorno** *m.* ornament,
  trimming
**aduana** *f.* custom-house

**aeronáutico,-a** aeronautic
**aeroplano** *m.* airplane
**aeropuerto** *m.* airport
**afeitarse** to shave
**aficionado** *m.* (fan of a sport)
**agencia** *f.* agency
**agente** *m.* agent
**agosto** *m.* August
**agradable** agreeable, pleasant
**agricultura** *f.* agriculture
**agricultor** *m.* farmer
**agua** *m.* water
  ... **caliente** hot water
  ... **fría** cold water
  ... **helada** ice water
**aguardiente** *m.* brandy
**águila** *m.* eagle
**aguja** *f.* needle
**ahora** now
  ... **mismo** right now,
  at once
**aire** *m.* air
**ajo** *m.* garlic
**ajustar** to adjust, to fit
**al** to the, at the, on the
**alemán,-a** German
**alemania** *f.* Germany
**albaricoque** *m.* apricot
**alcachofa** *f.* artichoke
**alcalde** *m.* mayor
**alcoba** *f.* bedroom
**alcohol** *m.* alcohol
**alegrarse** to be glad
**alfombra** *f.* rug
**algo** something, some
**algodón** *m.* cotton
**alguien** somebody
**alguno,-a** someone

alimento *m.* food
allí there
allá there, in that place
  por . . ., that way
almacén *m.* shop
almendra *f.* almond
almohada *f.* pillow
almorzar to have lunch
almuerzo *m.* lunch
alquilar to hire
alondra *f.* lark
alto loud, high, tall
alto stop (imp.)
amanecer *m.* daybreak
amapola *f.* poppy
amargo,-a bitter
amarillo,-a yellow
ambos,-as both
ambulancia *f.* ambulance
América del Sur *f.* South
  America
americano,-a American
amigo *m.* friend
amor *m.* love
amplio,-a wide
amueblado,-a furnished
ancho,-a broad, wide
andar to walk
angosto,-a narrow
animal *m.* animal
anoche last night
anochecer to become dark
ante, antes de before
anteayer day before yesterday
Antillas *f.* West Indies,
  Antilles
antiséptico,-a antiseptic
anual annual
anunciar to advertise,
  to announce
anuncio *m.* advertisement
año *m.* year
Año Nuevo *m.* New Year
apagar to put out, turn off
apenas scarcely
aperitivo *m.* aperitif
apetito *m.* appetite
apio *m.* celery
aplaudir to applaud

apostar to bet
apreciación *f.* appreciation
apreciar to appreciate
aprender to learn
apretado,-a tight
aprieto *m.* jam, tight spot
aprisa quick
apuesta *f.* bet
apurarse to hurry
apúrese hurry up (imp.)
aquí here
  por . . ., this way
arado *m.* plow
árbol *m.* tree
ardilla *f.* squirrel
armario *m.* closet, wardrobe
aromático,-a aromatic
arqueología *f.* archeology
arquitecto *m.* architect
arquitectura *f.* architecture
arranque automático
  self-starter
arrendar to rent, to lease
arriba above
arroz *m.* rice
arte *m.* art
artículos *m.* goods, articles
artificial artificial
artista *m.,f.* artist
artístico,-a artistic
asado,-a roasted, broiled
  bien . . . well done
asar to roast
ascender to rise, to climb
ascensor *m.* elevator
aseado,-a *m.* tidy
así so, thus
asiento *m.* seat
asistencia *f.* assistance,
  attendance
asistir to attend
aspirina *f.* aspirin
astringente *m.* astringent
asuntos *m.* affairs
asustarse to get frightened
atender to attend
atómico,-a atomic
atractivo,-a attractive
atrás backward, behind

**atrasado,-a** slow, backward
**aún** still, yet
**aunque** although
**aurora** f. dawn
**auto** m. automobile
**autobús** m. bus
**automóvil** m. automobile
**autoridad** f. authority
**avellana** f. hazelnut
**avena** f. oats
**avenida** f. avenue
**aviación** f. aviation
**avión** m. airplane, airliner
**¡ay!** alas!
**ayuntamiento** m. city hall
**ayer** yesterday
**azúcar** m. sugar
**azucarero** m. sugar bowl
**azucena** f. white lily
**azul** m. blue

## B

**bailar** to dance
**baile** m. dance
   **pista de . . .** dance floor
**bajar** to go or come down,
   to get off, to get down
**bajo,-a** low, soft, under
**balcón** m. balcony
**balde** m. bucket
   **de . . .** free
   **en . . .** in vain
**banco** m. bank
**banda** f. band
**bañarse** to bathe oneself
**baño** m. bath
   **cuarto de . . .** bathroom
**bañera** f. bathtub
**bar** m. bar
**barato,-a** cheap
**barco** m. ship
**barómetro** m. barometer
**basta** that is enough
**bastante** enough, quite,
   sufficiently
**barrer** to sweep
**batata** f. sweet potato
**baúl** m. trunk
**beber** to drink

**bebida** f. drink
   **. . . gaseosa** soft drink
**becerro** m. calf
**beisbol** m. baseball
**bermellón** m. vermilion
**bicicleta** f. bicycle
**bien** well
   **yo estoy . . .** I am well
**biftec** m. beefsteak
**billete** m. ticket, paper
   money
**biblioteca** f. library
**bien** well
**bisté** m. steak
**blanco,-a** white
**blando,-a** soft
**blusa** f. blouse
**bordado** m. embroidery
**bocina** f. automobile horn
**boleto** m. ticket
**bollo,** m. rolls (bread)
**bolsillo** m. pocket
**bolso,-a** purse
**bonito,-a** pretty
**bosque** m. woods
**bostezo** m. yawn
**botas** f., pl. boots
**botella** f. bottle
**botica** f. drugstore
**botón** m. button
**brazo** m. arm
**brisa** f. breeze
**buen** good
**bueno,-a** good
   **buena suerte** good luck
   **buenas noches** good night
   **buenas tardes** good
      afternoon
   **buenos días** good morning
**buey** m. ox
**bujía** f. spark plug
**burla** f. mockery, jest
   **de . . .** for fun
**burro** m. donkey
**buzón** m. mailbox

## C

**caballero** m. gentleman
**caballo** m. horse

**cabina** f. airplane cabin
**cabeza** f. head
**cable** m. cable
**cablegrama** m. cablegram
**cabra** f. goat
**cacao** m. cocoa
**cada** each
**caer** to fall
**caerse** to fall down
**café** m. coffee
   ... **con leche,** coffee with milk
**cafetera** f. coffee pot
**caja** f. box
**cajero,-a** cashier
**calcetines** m., pl. socks
**calefacción** f. heating
**calendario** m. calendar
**caliente** hot
**calabaza** f. pumpkin
**calle** f. street
**calor** m. warmth, heat
   **tengo** ... I am hot
**calzado** m. footwear
**cama** f. bed
**cámara** f. camera
**camarera** f. room maid
**camarero,-a** waiter, waitress
**camarote** m. cabin
**camarón** m. shrimp
**cambiar** to change
**cambiarse** to change (clothes)
**cambio** m. change, exchange
**caminar** to walk
**camino** m. road
**camión** m. truck, bus (Mex.)
**camioneta** station wagon
**camisa** f. shirt
**camiseta** f. undershirt
**campo** m. country, field
**canario** m. canary
**canasta** f. basket
**canción** f. song
**cansado,-a** tired
**cansarse** to get tired
**cantar** to sing
**cantidad** f. quantity
**canto** m. song
**cara** f. face

**carbón** m. carbon, coal
**carácter** m. character
**carcajada** f. burst of laughter
**cárcel** f. jail
**¡caramba!** inter. gracious! strange!
**carnaval** m. carnival
**carne** m. meat
   ... **de res** f. beef
**carnero** m. sheep, mutton
**carnicería** f. butcher shop
**caro,-a** expensive
**carreras de caballos** horseraces
**carretera** f. highway
**carretero** m. cart-driver
**carro** m. cart, car
**carta** f. letter
   **papel de** ... writing paper
**cartera** f. handbag, wallet
**casa** f. home, house
   ... **de huéspedes** boarding house
**casi** adv. almost
**casino** m. club
**castaña** f. chestnut
**castaño** m. chestnut tree, brown
**catarro** m. cold (illness)
**catedral** f. cathedral
**católico,-a** catholic
**catorce** fourteen
**cebada** f. barley
**cebolla** f. onion
**celebrar** to celebrate, to approve
**celebridad** f. celebrity
**celos** m. jealousy
**cena** f. supper
**cenar** to dine, to have supper
**centavo** m. cent
**centeno** m. rye
**centígrado** centigrade
**central** central
**céntrico,-a** central
**Centro América** f. Central America
**cepillarse** to brush

**cepillo** *m.* brush
   . . . **de dientes** toothbrush
**cerca** near
**cerdo** *m.* pig
**cereal** *m.* cereal
**cereza** *f.* cherry
**cerilla** *f.* match
**cero** *m.* zero
**cerrado,-a** closed
**cerrar** to close, shut
**cerveza** *f.* beer
**chaleco** *m.* vest
**chanclos** *m.* rubbers (shoes)
**chaqueta** *f.* coat, jacket
**cheque** *m.* check
   . . . **viajero** travelers check
**chicle** *m.* chewing gum
**chimenea** *f.* chimney
**chino,-a** Chinese
**chiquito,-a** small, little
**chiste** *m.* joke
**chistoso,-a** funny
**chocolate** *m.* chocolate
**chuleta** *f.* chop
   . . . **de puerco** pork chop
**cielo** *m.* sky
**ciento** hundred
   **por** . . . per cent
**cierto,-a** certain, sure
   **por** . . . incidentally
**ciervo** *m.* deer
**cigarrillo** *m.* cigarette
**cigarro** *m.* cigar
**cinco** *m.* five
**cincuenta** *m.* fifty
**cine** *m.* motion-picture
   theater
**cinta** *f.* ribbon
**cintura** *f.* waist, waistline
**cinturón** *m.* belt
**circo de toros** *m.* bullring
**ciruela** *f.* plum
**cita** *f.* appointment, date
**ciudad** *f.* city
**claro** clearly, pale, light
**clase** *f.* class, kind
   **primera** . . . first class
   **segunda** . . . second class
**clavel** *m.* carnation

**clima** *m.* climate
**clínica** *f.* clinic, doctor's office
**club** *m.* club
**cobre** *m.* copper
**coche** *m.* car
**cocina** *f.* kitchen
**cocinar** to cook
**cocinera** *f.* cook
**coco** *m.* cocoanut
**coctel** *m.* cocktail
**codo** *m.* elbow
**coger** to catch
**col** *f.* cabbage
**colcha** *f.* bedspread
**colchón** *m.* mattress
**colegio** *m.* school
**coliflor** *f.* cauliflower
**colonia** *f.* colony
**color** *m.* color
**colorado,-a** red
**comedor** *m.* dining room
**comenzar** to begin
**comer** to eat
**comercial** commercial
**comerciante** *m.* merchant
**comida** *f.* dinner, food
**como** as
**¿cómo?** how?
**cómoda** *f.* chest of drawers
**cómodo,-a** comfortable
**compañía** *f.* company
**comparación** *f.* comparison
**componer** to compose
   to repair
**compostura** *f.* repair
**compra** *f.* purchase
**comprar** to buy
   **¿dónde puedo** . . . **?** where
   can I buy?
**comprender** to understand
**comprendido,-a** understood
**compromiso** *m.* appointment,
   date
**comúnmente** commonly
**con** with
**concierto** *m.* concert
**conductor** *m.* driver,
   conductor
**conejo** *m.* rabbit

**confeti** *m.* confetti
**conforme** alike, suitable
  . . . a according to
**congelado,-a** frozen
**conmigo** with me
**conocer** to know (people,
  places), to be introduced to
**conocimiento** *m.* knowledge,
  bill of lading
**conque** so then, so that
**constar** to consist
**construir** to build,
  to construct
**contado,-a** rare
  **al . . .** (for) cash
**contar** to count
**contento-a** happy
**contestar** to answer
**contra** against
**contraer** to contract
**contrario,-a** contrary
  **al . . .** on the contrary
**consistir** to consist
**consulta** *f.* visit (doctor's),
  consultation
**convencer** to convince
**conveniente** convenient
**conversación** *f.* conversation
**copia** *f.* copy
**corbata** *f.* necktie
**cordero** *m.* lamb
**cordial** cordial
**corrección** *f.* correction
**correcto,-a** correct
**corredor** *m.* corridor, hall
**correo** *m.* mail
  **. . . aéreo** airmail
**correspondencia** *f.*
  correspondence
**corriente** *f.* current, draft
**cortar** to cut
**cortés** courteous
**cortesía** *f.* courtesy
**cortina** *f.* curtain
**corto,-a** short
  **muy . . .** too short
**cosa** *f.* thing
**coser** to sew
**cosecha** *f.* harvest

**cosmético** *m.* cosmetic
**costa** *f.* coast
**costar** to cost
**costillas** *f.* ribs
**costura** *f.* seam, sewing
**cotización** *f.* quotation
**crecer** to grow
**crecimiento** *m.* growth
**credencial** *f.* credential
**crédito** *m.* credit
  **a . . .** on credit
**creer** to believe, to think
  (opinion)
**crema** *f.* cream
**crepé** *m.* crepe
**criada** *f.* maid
**criminal** *m.* criminal
**cristal** *m.* crystal
**crudo,-a** raw
**cuaderno** *m.* notebook
**cuadra** *f.* block
**cuadrado** *m.* square
**cuadro** *m.* picture
**cuál** which
**cuales** which
**cualesquiera** whoever
**cualquier** any
**cualquiera** anyone, whatever
**cuando** when
**cuánto** how much, how many
**cuarenta** forty
**cuaresma** *f.* lent
**cuarto** *m.* quarter, fourth,
  room
**cuatro** four
**cubano-a,** Cuban
**cubierta** *f.* envelope
**cubierto** *m.* silverware
**cubrir** to cover
**cucaracha** *f.* cockroach
**cuchara** *f.* spoon
**cucharada** *f.* spoonful
**cucharita** *f.* teaspoon
**cuchilla** *f.* razor blade
**cuchillo** *m.* knife
**cuello** *m.* collar, neck
**cuenta** *f.* bill, restaurant
  check, account
**cuento** *m.* story

**cuervo** m. raven
**cuidado** caution
**cuidar** to take care of
**¡cuidado!** be careful!
**cumpleaños** m. birthday
**cuñada** f. sister-in-law
**cuñado** m. brother-in-law

## D

**dar** to give
**dátil** m. date
**de** from, of
**dé** give (imp.)
**debajo** beneath, under
**deber** ought, should, must
**debilidad** f. weakness
**decidir** to decide
**décimo,-a** tenth
**decir** to say, to tell
**decisión** f. decision
**declaración** f. declaration
**decorar** to decorate
**dedo** m. finger
**deducción** f. deduction
**defectivo,-a** defective
**defecto** m. defect
**defender** to defend
**dejar** to leave, to allow, to let
**del** of the, from the, about the
**delante** before
**delgado** thin
**delicioso,-a** delicious
**demasiado** too much
**démelo** give it to me
**dentista** m.,f. dentist
**dentro** inside
　. . . **de** within
**departamento** m. apartment, department
**depositado** deposited
**depositar** to deposit
**derecha** f. right
**derecho** straight, straight ahead
**derretir** to melt
**desabrido,-a** tasteless
**desagradable** disagreeable
**desalquilado,-a** free, unhired, unrented

**desamueblado,-a** unfurnished
**desaparecer** to disappear
**desastroso,-a** disastrous
**desayuno** m. breakfast
**descansar** to rest
**descender** to descend, to go down
**descompuesto,-a** out of order
**descontar** to discount
**describiendo** describing
**describir** to describe
**descubrir** to discover
**descripción** f. description
**descriptivo,-a** descriptive
**descuento** m. discount
**desde** from
**desear** to wish
**desenvolver** to unwrap
**deseo** m. desire
**deshacerse** to get rid of
**desinfectante** m. disinfectant
**desobedecer** to disobey
**despacio** slowly
**despacho** m. office, despatch, shipment
**despedirse** to take leave of
**despertar** to wake up
**después** after
**desvestirse** to undress
**desvío** m. detour
**detener** to detain
**detestar** to detest
**detrás** behind
**devolver** to return (a thing)
**día** m. day
**diagnóstico** m. diagnosis
**diamante** m. diamond
**diario** m. daily, journal
**diccionario** m. dictionary
**diciembre** m. December
**diecinueve** nineteen
**dieciocho** eighteen
**dieciséis** sixteen
**diecisiete** seventeen
**diente** m. tooth
**diez** ten
**diferencia** f. difference
**diferente** different
**difícil** difficult

dificultades *f.* troubles,
  difficulties
dígame tell me
digestible digestible
digestión *f.* digestion
digo I say, tell
dije I said, told
dinero *m.* money
Dios God
diplomacia *f.* diplomacy
diplomático,-a diplomat
dirección *f.* address, direction
directo,-a direct
directorio *m.* directory
disco *m.* phonograph record
discurso *m.* speech
discusión *f.* discussion
discutir to discuss, to argue
dispensar to excuse
  dispénseme excuse me
distancia *f.* distance
distribución *f.* distribution
distribuir to distribute
dividir to divide
diversión *f.* entertainment
divertirse to have a good time
dividido divided
doble double
doce twelve
docena *f.* dozen
doctor,-a doctor
dólar *m.* dollar
doler to hurt
dolor *m.* ache
domingo *m.* Sunday
donde where
dormir to sleep
dormirse to go to sleep
dormitorio *m.* bedroom,
  dormitory
dos two
doy I give
duda *f.* doubt, uncertainty
dudar to doubt
dueño,-a owner
dulce sweet
durable durable
duradero,-a durable, lasting
durante during

durar to last
duro,-a tough, hard

**E**

¡Ea! Well!
echar to pour, to throw,
  to dump, to put out
edificio *m.* building
efectivo,-a effective
  hacer . . . to cash
ejotes *m.* string beans
el the
él he
electricidad *f.* electricity
eléctrico,-a electric
elefante *m.* elephant
elegante elegant
elevado,-a high
elevador *m.* elevator
ella she
embarcar to sail, embark
emborracharse to get drunk
embrague *m.* clutch
emergencia *f.* emergency
en in, on, at
encaje *m.* lace
encerrar to lock in
encima above, overhead
  . . . de on, upon
encender to light, to burn
  . . . la luz to put on the light
encontrar to meet, to find,
  to encounter
encuentro *m.* encounter
enero *m.* January
enfermedad *f.* sickness
enfermarse to get sick
enfermo,-a sick
  estoy . . . I am sick
enfriarse to get cold
enojado,-a angry
ensalada *f.* salad
enseñar to teach, to show
entender to understand
entendido understood
enterarse to find out
yo entiendo I understand
entonces then

**entrar** to enter, to go in, to come in
**entre** between, among
**entrega** f. delivery
**entregar** to deliver
**entretener** to entertain
**entusiasmarse** to get enthusiastic
**entusiasmo** enthusiasm
**envío** m. shipment
**envolver** to wrap
**envuelto,-a** wrapped
**equipaje** m. baggage
**equivalente** equivalent
**equivocarse** to make a mistake
**era** was, were, used to be, it was, it used to be
**error** m. error
**es** is, are, it is
**escalera** f. staircase, ladder
**escalones** stairs, steps
**escribiendo** writing
**escritorio** m. desk
**escuela** f. school
**escultura** f. sculpture
**esencial** essential
**eso,-a** that
**espacioso,-a** spacious, roomy
**espalda** f. back
**España** f. Spain
**español,-a** Spaniard, Spanish
**espárragos** m. asparagus
**especial** special
**especialmente** specially
**esperado** hoped, waited, expected
**esperanza** f. hope
**esperar** to hope, to wait, to expect
**espinaca** f. spinach
**esposa** f. wife
**esposo** m. husband
**esponja** f. sponge
**esquina** f. corner
**esta** f. this
**ésta** f. this one
**está** is, (you) are
　¿**cómo** ... **usted?** how are you?

**establecer** to establish
**estación** f. station, season
　... **de gasolina** gas station
**estacionar** to park
**estadio** m. stadium
**estado** m. state, been
**Estados Unidos** m. United States
**estamos** we are
**estampilla** f. stamp
**están** they are, you are
**estaño** m. tin
**estar** to be
**estatua** f. statue
**este,-a** this
**este** m. east
**éste** this one
**estilo** m. style
**estómago** m. stomach
**estornudo** m. sneeze
**estos** m. these
**estoy** I am
**estrecho,-a** tight, narrow
**estudiante** student
**estúpido,-a** stupid
**estuve** I was
**evadir** to evade, avoid
**exactamente** exactly
**exacto,-a** exact
**exageración** f. exaggeration
**exagerar** to exaggerate
**examinar** to examine
**excavación** f. excavation
**excessivo,-a** excessive
**excepto** except
**excúseme** excuse me
**exhibición** f. exhibition
**exigir** to demand
**existencia** f. existence
**éxito** m. success
**experiencia** f. experience
**explicar** to explain
**exportar** to export
**expresar** to express
**exterior** exterior, outside room
**extranjero,-a** foreign, foreigner
**extraño,-a** strange, foreign

## F

**fábrica** *f.* factory
**facial** facial
**fácil** easy
**facilidad** *f.* facility, ease
**facturar** to check, to invoice
**faja** *f.* girdle
**falda** *f.* skirt
**falta** *f.* lack, want
**faltar** to lack, to miss
**famoso,-a** famous
**fango** *m.* mud
**farmacia** *f.* drugstore
**familia** *f.* family
**favor** *m.* favor
**fealdad** *f.* ugliness
**fabrero** *m.* February
**fecha** *f.* date
**felicidad** *f.* happiness
**felicitar** to congratulate
**feo,-a** ugly
**ferrocarril** *m.* railroad
**fervor** *m.* fervor, enthusiasm
**festival** *f.* festival
**festividad** *f.* festivity, feast
**fieltro** *m.* felt
**fiesta** *f.* feast
    **día de . . .** holiday
**fiebre** *f.* fever, temperature
**filete** *m.* cutlet
**fin** *m.* end, conclusion
    **al . . .** at last
    **por . . .** at last
    **en . . .** finally
**finalmente** finally
**firma** *f.* firm, concern
**firmar** to sign
**flor** *f.* flower
**florista** *m.,f.* florist
**flotando** floating
**flotar** to float
**fluctuación** fluctuation
**fogón** *m.* fireplace, stove
**fonógrafo** *m.* phonograph
**formal** formal
**formar** to form
**fortuna** *f.* fortune
**fósforo** *m.* match

**foto** *f.* photograph
**fotografía** *f.* photograph
**fotografiar** to photograph
**fracasar** to fail
**fracaso** *m.* failure
**fracción** *f.* fraction
**frambuesa** *f.* raspberry
**francés,-sa** French,
    Frenchman, Frenchwoman
**Francia** *f.* France
**frecuentemente** frequently
**fregadero** *m.* sink
**freír** to fry
**frenos** *m.* automobile brakes
**frente** in front, opposite
**fresa** *f.* strawberry
**fresco** *m.* cool, fresh
**fríjoles** *m.* beans
**frío,-a** cold
    **tengo . . .** I am cold
**frito,-a** fried
**fruta** *f.* fruit
**fuente** *f.* platter, tray,
    fountain
**fuera** without, outside
**fuerte** *m.* fort
**fuí** I was, I went
**fumar** to smoke
**funeral** *m.* funeral
**futbol** *m.* football (soccer)

## G

**gabardina** *f.* gabardine,
    raincoat
**galleta** *f.* cracker, cookie
**gallina** *f.* hen
**gallo** *m.* cock
    **pelea de gallos** cock fight
**gallera** *f.* cock pit
**ganado** *m.* cattle
**ganancia** *f.* profit
**ganso** *m.* goose
**ganas** *f.* desire, yen
**garage** *m.* garage
**gas** *m.* gas
**gasolina** *f.* gasoline
**gato** *m.* cat
**gaveta** *f.* locker
**generador** *m.* generator

**general** *m.* general
**generalmente** generally, ordinarily
**género** *m.* material, gender
**gente** *f.* people
**ginebra** *f.* gin
**girar** to spin
**giro** *m.* draft
**gloria** *f.* glory
**golondrina** *f.* swallow
**gobierno** *m.* government
**golf** *m.* golf
**goma** *f.* rubber
**gordo,-a** fat
**gorra** *f.* cap
**gozo** *m.* joy
**gracia** *f.* grace, charm
**gracias** *f.* thank you, thanks
**gracioso,-a** graceful, amusing
**grande** large, big
**grado** *m.* degree
**granja** *f.* farm
**grano** *m.* grain
**gratis** gratis, free
**grave** grave, very ill
**gris** *m.* gray
**gritar** to shout, to scream
**grito** *m.* shout, scream
**gruesa** *f.* gross
**guagua** *f.* bus (Cuba)
**guantes** gloves
**guapo,-a** handsome
**guías del viajero** road map
**guisado** *m.* stew
**guisantes** *m.* peas
**guitarra** *f.* guitar
**gustar** to like
  **si gusta** if you please
**gusto** *m.* taste, pleasure

## H

**ha** you have (he, she, it) has
**haber** to be
**había** there was, there were, was there?, were there? there used to be, did there used to be?
**habichuelas** *f.* beans

**habitación** *f.* room, chamber
**habitantes** inhabitants
**habla** (he, she) speaks (you) speak
**hablado** talked
**hablar** to speak
**hacer** to do
**hacia** toward
**hacienda** *f.* ranch, large farm
**hambre** *m.* hunger
  **tengo . . .** I am hungry
**hasta** up to, until
  **. . . la vista, . . . luego** until we meet again
**hay** there is, there are
  **. . . que** it is necessary
**helada** *f.* frost
**helado** *m.* ice cream
**helar** to freeze
**hélice** *f.* propeller
**heno** *m.* hay
**hermana** *f.* sister
**hermano** *m.* brother
**hermoso,-a** beautiful
**hermosura** *f.* beauty
**hervir** to boil
**hielo** *m.* ice
**higo** *m.* fig
**hija** *f.* daughter
**hijo** *m.* son
**hilo** *m.* thread
**hipo** *m.* hiccough
**historia** *f.* history
**hogar** *m.* home
**hoja** *f.* sheet, leaf
**¡Hola!** Hello!
**hombre** *m.* man
**hombro** *m.* shoulder
**hora** *f.* hour, time
**honor** *m.* honor
**horario** *m.* hour hand, timetable
**horno** *m.* oven
**hortelano** *m.* farmer, gardener
**hospital** *m.* hospital
**hospitalidad** *f.* hospitality
**hoy** today

**hubo** there was, there were, was there? were there?

**huerta** f. orchard

**huevo** m. egg
... **duro** hard boiled egg
... **frito** fried egg
... **pasado por agua** soft boiled egg

**humor** m. humor

**húngaro,-a** Hungarian

**humedad** f. humidity

# I

**iba** (he, she, it) went, used to go, was going

**idea** f. idea

**idioma** m. language

**iglesia** f. church

**ignorancia** f. ignorance

**ignorante** ignorant

**igual** equal

**ilegal** illegal

**ilustración** m. illustration

**imaginación** m. imagination

**imitación** f. imitation

**impaciencia** f. impatience

**impermeable** m. raincoat, waterproof

**importante** important

**importar** to import

**importe** m. amount, value

**imposibilidad** f. impossibility

**imposible** impossible

**imprimir** to print

**impuesto** m. duty (tax)

**incluír** to include

**incompetente** incompetent

**incorrecto,-a** incorrect

**independencia** f. independence

**indigestión** f. indigestion

**indispuesto,-a** indisposed

**indolente** indolent

**industrial** industrial

**infección** f. infection

**influencia** f. influence

**informar** to inform

**ingeniero** m. engineer

**Inglaterra** f. England

**inicial** initial

**inmenso,-a** immense

**inocular** to inoculate

**insecto** m. insect

**insignificante** insignificant

**instalar** to install

**instante** m. instant

**insultar** to insult

**insulto** m. insult

**inteligente** intelligent

**interior** m. interior

**internacional** international

**interrumpir** to interrupt

**íntimamente** intimately

**íntimo,-a** intimate

**itinerario** m. timetable

**introducción** f. introduction

**invierno** m. winter

**invitación** f. invitation

**invitado,-a** guest, visitor

**invitar** to invite

**ir** to go

**irse** to go away

**italiano,-a** Italian

**itinerario** m. itinerary

**izquierda** f. left

# J

**jardín** m. garden

**jarra** f. pitcher

**jabalí** m. boar

**jabón** m. soap

**jabonera** f. soap dish

**jamás** never

**jamón** m. ham

**jefe** m. chief, boss

**jornales** wages

**joven** young

**joyería** f. jewelry store

**judío,-a** Jewish

**juego** m. game
**hacer** ... to match

**jueves** m. Thursday

**jugar** to play (a game), to gamble

**jugo** m. juice

**juguete** m. toy

# Why We Make This Generous Offer

There are three important reasons why the Institute for Language Study is pleased to make this special Free Record and Sample Lesson offer:

*First,* never before have there been so many fascinating opportunities open to those who speak foreign languages fluently. Besides the cultural and travel benefits, there are many practical dollars-and-cents advantages—and an ever-increasing number of interesting, well-paying jobs.

## The Natural Method

*Second,* our long experience in the language field has convinced us that the "learn-by-listening" method is the fastest, most convenient and most effective one. It enables you to learn *naturally*—the way you learned English as a child. You acquire a perfect accent and perfect grammar—because that's all you hear.

## Just Listen—and Learn

*Finally,* our professional standing in the field of languages has enabled us to make these generous arrangements with one of the foremost language schools—the inventors of the "learn-by-listening" method. And we are pleased to provide this service for those of our students who want to speak and understand a foreign language "like a native."

There is no obligation and *no salesman will call.* Just mail the card TODAY for your FREE Record.

## What Others Say:

**Institute for Language Study**
**71 Plymouth Street, Montclair, N.J. 07042**

## INSTITUTE FOR LANGUAGE STUDY Dept. HVP/RC
71 Plymouth Street, Montclair, N. J. 07042

Gentlemen:

Please have the originators of the famous "learn-by-listening" method send me, FREE, the Sample Record and Lesson in the one language checked below—also information which describes fully the complete course and method.

▲ **Please check FREE Language Recording and Lesson you wish:**

☐ Spanish  ☐ French  ☐ German  ☐ Italian  ☐ Brazilian-Portuguese
☐ Russian  ☐ Japanese  ☐ Modern Greek  ☐ English (for Spanish-or
☐ Arabic                                      Portuguese-speaking people)

▲ **Check one:** ☐ RECORD or ☐ CASSETTE

Name _____

Address _____

City _____ State _____

Zip Code _____ Phone _____

BK **HVP** /54321

# BUSINESS REPLY CARD

FIRST CLASS    PERMIT NO. 1103    Montclair, N.J.

POSTAGE WILL BE PAID BY ADDRESSEE

**Institute for Language Study**
**71 Plymouth Street**
**Montclair, NJ 07042**

**juicio** m. judgment
**julio** m. July
**junio** m. June
**junto** near, close
**juntos,-as** together
**justicia** f. justice
**justillo** m. brassiere
**justo-a** just, fair
**juventud** f. youth

## K

**kilo** f. kilo, kilogram

## L

**la** the
**lago** m. lake
**lágrima** f. tear
**lámpara** f. lamp
**lana** f. wool
**lancha** f. launch, boat
**lápiz** m. pencil
**largo,-a** long
  **muy ...** too long
**lastimarse** to hurt oneself
**lavandería** f. laundry
**lavarse** to wash (oneself)
**lavabo** m. wash basin
**lavar** to wash
**leal** loyal
**lección** f. lesson
**lechuga** f. lettuce
**leche** f. milk
**leer** to read
**legal** legal
**legumbre** f. vegetable
**lejos** far
  **¿qué tan ... es?** how far
  is it?
**lengua** f. tongue
**lentejas** f. lentils
**león** m. lion
**leopardo** m. leopard
**letra** f. letter
**letrero** m. sign
**levantar** to raise, to lift,
  pick up
  **levantarse** to get up
**liar** to tie

**librería** f. bookstore
**libro** m. book
**liebre** f. hare
**lima** f. lime
**limón** m. lemon
**limonada** f. lemonade
**limpiar** to clean
**limpiavidrios** m. windshield
  wiper
**limpio-a** clean
**lino** m. linen
**lío** m. a scrape, trouble
**lirio** m. lily
**lista** f. list
  **... de platos** bill of fare
**listo,-a** ready
**llama** f. llama
**llamar** to call
**llamarse** to be called (name)
**llanta** f. tire
**llave** f. key
**llegada** f. arrival
**llegar** to arrive
  **al ...** upon arrival
**llegué** I arrived, got here,
  got there
**llevar** to wear, to carry, to take
  (someone or something
  some place)
**llorar** to cry
**llover** to rain
**lluvia** f. rain
**lo** m. it, him
**lobo** m. wolf
**local** local
**loco,-a** crazy
**lodo** m. mud
**lotería** f. lottery
**lubricación** f. lubrication
**lubricante** m. lubricant
**lubricar** to lubricate
**luego** later
  **hasta ...** so long
**lugar** m. place
**lujo** m. luxury
**luna** f. moon
**lunes** m. Monday
**luz** f. light

# M

**madera** *f.* wood
**madre** *f.* mother
**madrugada** *f.* dawn
**maestro,-a** teacher
**mal** badly, ill
**maleta** *f.* suitcase
**malo,-a** bad
**mamá** *f.* mom, mama
**mandado** *m.* errand
**mandar** to send
**manecillas** hands (of a watch)
**manejar** to drive, to manage
**manga** *f.* sleeve
**mano** *f.* hand
**mansión** *f.* mansion
**mantel** *m.* tablecloth
**mantequilla** *f.* butter
**manzana** *f.* apple
**mañana** *f.* morning,
   tomorrow
   **... por la ...** tomorrow
      morning
**mapa** *m.* map
**máquina** *f.* machine
   **... de escribir** typewriter
**maquinaria** *f.* works,
   machinery
**marcha** *f.* march
   **en ...** it is starting
**marearse** to get seasick, airsick
**mareo** *m.* dizziness
**marina** *f.* navy
**martes** *m.* Tuesday
**marzo** *m.* March
**más** more
   **... que** more than
**masa** *f.* bread, dough
**matriculación** *f.* registration
**matricular** to matriculate,
   to register
**mayo** *m.* May
**mayor** main, major, eldest
**mazorca** *f.* ear of corn
**mí** me, myself
**mecánico,-a** mechanic
**medianoche** *f.* midnight
**mediante** by means of

**medias** stockings
**medicinal** medicinal
**médico** *m.* doctor
**medicina** *f.* medicine
**medio** means, middle, half
   **por ... de** by means of
**mediodía** *m.* midday, noon
**medir** to measure
**mejor** better
**mejorarse** to get better
**melocotón** *m.* peach
**melón** *m.* melon
**memoria** *f.* memory
**menos** but, except, less
   **al ... at** least
**mentir** to lie
**mentira** *f.* lie
**menú** *m.* menu
**menudo,-a** small, little,
   minute
   **a ...** often
**mercado** *m.* market place
**mercancía** *f.* merchandise
**mermelada** *f.* marmalade
**mes** *m.* month
   **por ...** by the month
**mesa** *f.* table
**metal** *m.* metal
**mexicano,-a** Mexican
**mi** my
**mídaselo** try it on (imp.)
**miedo** *m.* fear
**miel de abejas** *f.* honey
**miércoles** *m.* Wednesday
**mil** thousand
**mina** *f.* mine
**mineral** *m.* mineral
**minutero** *m.* minute hand
**minuto** *m.* minute
   **espere un ...** wait a minute
**mío,-a** mine
**mire** look (imp.)
**mismo,-a** same
**mis** my
**mitad** *f.* half
**moda** *f.* fashion, style
**moderno,-a** modern
**modista** *f.* dressmaker
**modo** *m.* manner

molestar  to bother
momento  m. moment
moneda  f. money, currency
monetario,-a  monetary
mono  m. monkey
morder  to bite
moreno,-a  brunette
mosaico  m. mosaic, tile
mosco  m. fly
mostaza  f. mustard
mostrar  to show
motor  m. motor
motorista  m.,f. motorist
moviendo  moving
muchacha  f. girl
muchacho  m. boy
mucho,-a  much
muchos,-as  many
mudar  to move
mueble  m. furniture
muelle  m. pier
muestra  f. sample
mujer  f. woman
mula  f. mule
mundo  m. world
mural  m. mural
museo  m. museum
música  f. music
muy  very
    . . . bien  very well

## N

nabo  m. turnip
nacionalidad  f. nationality
nacer  to be born
nacimiento  m. birth
nación  f. nation
nacional  national
nada  nothing
nadar  to swim
nadie  nobody
naranja  f. orange
    jugo de . . . m. orange juice
natilla  f. custard
nativo,-a  f. native
natural  natural
naturalmente  naturally
Navidad  f. Christmas

necesario,-a  necessary
necesidad  f. necessity
necesitar  to need
negativo  negative
negligente  negligent
negocio  m. business
negro,-a  black
nena  f. baby girl
nene  m. baby boy
nervioso,-a  nervous
nevar  to snow
ni . . . ni  neither . . . nor
nieta  f. granddaughter
nieto  m. grandson
nieve  f. snow
ninguno  no one
niña  f. girl
niñez  f. childhood
niño,-a  child
no  no
noble  noble
noche  f. evening, night
    esta . . . tonight
Noche Buena  f. Christmas
    Eve
nombre  m. name
norte  m. north
Norte América  f. North
    America
norte americano,-a  North
    American
nos  us, ourselves
nosotros,-as  we, us
nota  f. note
notar  to note, to notice
notario  m. notary public
noticiario  m. newsreel
noticias  f. news
noventa  ninety
noviembre  m. November
nublado,-a  cloudy
nuestro,-a  our, ours
nueve  nine
nuevo,-a  new
nuez  f. nut
número  m. number
numeroso,-a  numerous
nunca  never

# O

o either, or
obtener to obtain
ocasión f. occasion
occidente m. west, occident
oculista m.,f. oculist
ocupación f. occupation
ocupado,-a busy
ocho eight
ochenta eighty
octubre m. October
ocupar to occupy
ocurrir to occur
odiar to hate
odio m. hatred
ofender to offend
ofendido,-a offended
ofensivo,-a offensive
oficial official
oficina f. office
ofrecer to offer
oiga listen, hear (imp.)
oír to hear
ola f. wave
olfato m. smell
olivo m. olive-tree
olvidar to forget
once eleven
onza f. ounce
ópera f. opera
operador m. operator
operación f. operation
opinión f. opinion
órdenes orders
    a sus . . . at your service
ordinario,-a ordinary
oreja f. ear
oriente east, orient
original original
orquesta f. orchestra
orquídea f. orchid
oro m. gold
oscuro,-a dark
oso m. bear
ostra f. oyster
otoño m. autumn
otro,-a other
    uno u . . . one or the other

otros,-as others, other
oveja f. sheep
oye hear, listen (imp.)

# P

paciencia f. patience
paciente patient
padre m. father
padres m. parents
pagar to pay
pago m. payment
país m. country
pagué I paid
paja f. straw
pájaro m. bird
pala f. shovel
palabra f. word
palacio m. palace
palma f. palm tree
palmeras f. palm trees
paloma f. dove
pan m. bread
pantalla f. movie screen,
    lamp shade
pantalones m. trousers
paño m. cloth
pañuelo m. handkerchief
papa f. potato
papel m. paper
papelería f. stationery store
paquete m. package
par m. pair, couple
para for, to
parabrisa m. windshield
paraguas m. umbrella
pararse to stand up, to stop
pardo brown
pare stop (imp.)
parecer to appear, seem
parecerse to resemble
pared f. wall
pargo m. red snapper
parientes m. relatives
parque m. park
parqueadero m. parking
parrilla f. grill
pasa f. raisin

**pasado,-a** past
  ... **mañana** day after tomorrow
**pasaje** *m.* ticket
**pasar** to pass
**Pascua** *f.* Easter
**pasear** to take a walk, a ride
  **dar un paseo** to go for a walk, ride
**pasta** *f.* paste
**pastel** *m.* pie
**pastor** *m.* shepherd
**patio** *m.* inner court
**patriótico,-a** patriotic
**patrón** *m.* boss, pattern
**pato** *m.* duck
**pavimento** *m.* pavement
**pavo** *m.* turkey
**pedir** to order, to ask
**peine** *m.* comb
**película** *f.* film
**peligro** *m.* danger
**peligroso,-a** dangerous
**pelo** *m.* hair
**penicilina** penicillin
**pensamiento** *m.* thought, pansy
**pensar** to think
**pensión** *f.* pension, boarding house
**peón** *m.* peasant
**peor** worse
**pepino** *m.* cucumber
**pequeño,-a** small
  **muy ... ,-a** too small
**pera** *f.* pear
**perder** to lose
**perdiz** *f.* partridge
**perezoso,-a** lazy
**perfecto-a** perfect
**perfume** *m.* perfume
**periódico** *m.* newspaper
**permanente** permanent, permanent wave
**permítame** allow me
**permitido,-a** permitted
**permitir** to allow
**pero** but
**perro** *m.* dog

**personal** personal
**personalmente** personally, in person
**persuadir** to persuade
**pesar** to weigh
**pesarse** to weigh yourself
**pescado** *m.* fish
**pescar** to fish
**peso** *m.* weight, peso
**petróleo** *m.* petroleum, crude oil
**picante** hot, spicy, piquant
**pie** *m.* foot
**piedra** *f.* stone, jewel
**piel** *f.* leather, hide
**pierna** *f.* leg
**pieza** *f.* room, piece, part
**píldora** *f.* pill
**piloto** *m.* pilot
**pimienta** *f.* pepper
**pintar** to paint
**pintura** *f.* painting
**piña** *f.* pineapple
**pipa** *f.* pipe
**piscina** *f.* swimming pool
**piso** *m.* floor
  ... **bajo** ground floor
**placer** *m.* pleasure
**plan** *m.* plan
**planchar** to iron
**planta** *m.* plant
**plátano** *m.* banana
**plato** *m.* dish, plate
**playa** *f.* beach
**plaza** *f.* square, market
**pluma** *f.* pen
**pobre** poor
**poco,-a** little
**poder** to be able
**policía** *m.* policeman
**política** *f.* politics
**pollo** *m.* chicken
**polvo** *m.* powder
**poner** to put, to set
**ponerse** to put on
**ponqué** *m.* cake
**popular** popular
**populoso,-a** densely populated
**por** by, for, through

porque because
  por qué why
portezuela f. car door
posible possible
posiblemente possibly
posición f. position
positivo,-a positive
postal f. postal
postre m. dessert
postrero,-a last
practicar to practice
práctico,-a practical
precio m. price
precioso,-a precious
predilecto,-a preferred,
  favorite
preferir to prefer
pregunta f. question
preguntar to ask
premio m. prize
preocupada,-a worried
preocupar to worry
preparar to prepare
presentar to present,
  to introduce
presente m. present
prestar to lend
primavera f. Spring
primero,-a first
primo,-a cousin
principal principal
prisa f. haste
  de ... quickly, fast
  dése ... hurry (imp.)
probablemente probably
probar to taste, to prove,
  to test
proceder to proceed
producir to produce
producto m. product
profesión f. profession
programa m. program
progresar to progress
progreso m. progress
prohibir to prohibit
  prohibida la entrada keep
  out
prometer to promise

pronto soon, fast
  de ... suddenly
pronunciación f.
  pronunciation
pronunciar to pronounce
propina f. tip
propio,-a proper, own
protección f. protection
protestante Protestant
protestar to protest
provincia f. province
provincial provincial
próximo,-a next
prueba f. proof
publicación f. publication
público,-a public
pueblo m. town
puente m. bridge
puerco m. pork, pig
puerta f. door
pues since, for
pulsera f. bracelet
  reloj de ... wristwatch
pulso m. pulse
puerto m. port
punto m. point, dot
  en ... exactly
puntual punctual
puño m. cuff, fist
puro m. cigar

# Q

que that, which
qué what, which
  ... es eso? what is that
quebrar to break
quedarse to stay, to remain
quejido m. groan
querer to want, to love
queso m. cheese
quién who
quienquiera whoever
quince fifteen
quizá perhaps

# R

rábano m. radish
racial racial
radiador m. radiator

radio radio
rancho *m.* ranch
rápidamente rapidly
rápido,-a rapid
rascarse to scratch
rata *f.* rat
ratón *m.* mouse
raro,-a rare, odd
   rara vez seldom
rayón *m.* rayon
razón *f.* reason
realizar to make, perform,
   realize
recibidor *m.* living room
receta *f.* prescription
recibir to receive
recibo *m.* receipt
reciente recent
reclamación *m.* complaint
reclamar to complain
recomendación *f.*
   recommendation
recomendar to recommend
reconocer to recognize
recordar to remember
recreación *f.* recreation
recuerdo *m.* souvenir
reducir to reduce
refajo *m.* slip
reflector *m.* reflector
refrescar to refresh
refrigeración *f.* refrigeration
refrigeradora *f.* refrigerator
región *f.* region
registración *f.* registration
registrar to register
regresar to return
regularidad *f.* regularity
reírse to laugh
relación *f.* relation
relativo,-a relative
relámpago *m.* lightning
reloj *m.* watch
relojería *f.* watch shop
relojero *m.* watchmaker
remendar to mend
remolacha *f.* beet
renta *f.* rent, income
reparar to repair

repente, de suddenly
repetir to repeat
repollo *m.* cabbage
requerir to require
resbalarse to slip, to slide
resfriado *m.* cold (illness)
resfriarse to catch cold
residencial residential
respetable respectable
responsable responsible
restaurante *m.* restaurant
resto *m.* rest
   el ... the rest
restricción *f.* restriction
reunión *f.* reunion
revolver to mix
revuelto scrambled
ridículo,-a ridiculous
río *m.* river
risa *f.* laughter
robar to steal, to rob
robo *m.* theft, robbery
robustez *m.* robustness
rogar to beg
rojo,-a red
rollo *m.* roll film
romántico,-a romantic
romper to tear, to break
ron *m.* rum
roncar to snore
ropa *f.* clothes
   ... interior underwear
rosa *f.* rose
rosario *m.* rosary
rosbif *m.* roast beef
rubio,-a blond
ruborizarse to blush
rueda *f.* wheel
rumba *f.* rumba
rumor *m.* rumor
rural *m.* rural
ruso Russian
ruta *f.* route

## S

sábado *m.* Saturday
sábana *f.* sheet
saber to know
sacacorchos *m.* corkscrew

saco *m.* coat
sal *f.* salt
sala *f.* living room
salado,-a salty
salida *f.* departure, exit
salario *m.* salary
salir to leave
salsa *f.* sauce, dressing
saltar to jump
salud *f.* health
saludar to greet
saludo *m.* greeting
salvar to save
sandía *f.* watermelon
sandwich *m.* sandwich
sarape *m.* Mexican blanket
sardina *f.* sardine
sastre *m.* tailor
sastrería *f.* tailor shop
satisfacer to satisfy
secarse to dry (yourself)
sección *f.* section
secretario,-a secretary
sed thirst
   tengo ... I am thirsty
seda *f.* silk
sedativo *m.* sedative
seis six
según according to
segundo,-a second
seguro,-a safe
seguro *m.* insurance
selección *f.* selection
seleccionar to select, choose
sello *m.* stamp, seal
semana *f.* week
   por ... by the week
   ... Santa Holy Week
   esta ... this week
sembrar to sow
sentar to sit, to fit
señalar to show, point
señor *m.* Mr., sir, gentleman
señorita *f.* Miss, young girl
sentarse to sit down
sentir to feel, to be sorry
septiembre *m.* September
séptimo,-a seventh
ser to be

serpiente *f.* serpent
servicio *m.* service
servilleta *f.* napkin
servir to serve
seta *f.* mushroom
si if
sí yes
siempre always
   ... que whenever
siento I feel
   lo ... I am sorry
siete seven
siglo *m.* century
silencio silence
silla *f.* chair
sillón *m.* armchair
simpático,-a charming,
   sympathetic
simple single, simple
simplicidad *f.* simplicity
sin without
sinceridad *f.* sincerity
síntomas *m.* symptoms
sistema *m.* system
sitio *m.* place, location
situación *f.* situation
situar to situate
sobre on, upon
sobre *m.* envelope
sobrina *f.* niece
sobrino *m.* nephew
sociable sociable
social social
sociedad *f.* society
sofá *m.* sofa
sofocante suffocating
sol *m.* sun
solo,-a alone
sollozo *m.* sob
solución *f.* solution
sombra *f.* shade
sombrero *m.* hat
sombrerería *f.* hat store
soñar to dream
sonreírse to smile
sopa *f.* soup
sorprender to surprise
soso,-a insipid, tasteless
suave soft

**subir** to enter, to go up
**suburbio** *m.* suburb
**sucesivamente** successively
**sucio,-a** dirty
**sucursal** *f.* branch
**sudar** to perspire
**suegra** *f.* mother-in-law
**suegro** *m.* father-in-law
**suela** *f.* sole
**suelo** *m.* ground
**sueño** *m.* dream
**suerte** *f.* luck
**suéter** *m.* sweater
**suficiente** sufficient, enough
**supuesto** assumed, supposed
  **por . . .** of course
**sur** *m.* south
**Sur América** *f.* South America
**suspiro** *m.* sigh
**suyo** yours, his, hers

## T

**tabaco** *m.* tobacco
**tabla** *f.* board
**tacto** *m.* touch
**tacón** *m.* heel
**talla** *f.* size
**talle** *m.* waist
**talón** *m.* baggage check
**tal vez** maybe
**también** also
**tampoco** neither
**tango** *m.* tango
**tanque** *m.* tank
**tanto,-a** as much, so much
**tantos,-as** as many, so many
**taquilla** *f.* box office
**tarde** *f.* afternoon, late
  **más . . .** later
**tarea** *f.* task
**tarjeta** *f.* card
**taxi** *m.* taxicab
**taza** *f.* cup
**té** *m.* tea
**teatro** *m.* theater
**tela** *f.* fabric
**telefonear** to telephone
**teléfono** *m.* telephone

**telegrafista** *m.f.* telegraph
  operator
**telegrama** *m.* telegram
**televisión** *f.* television
**temer** to fear
**temperatura** *f.* temperature
**temprano** early
**tenedor** *m.* fork
**tener** to have
**tenis** *m.* tennis
**tercero,-a** third
**terciopelo** *m.* velvet
**terminado,-a** finished
**terminar** to finish
**termómetro** *m.* thermometer
**ternera** *f.* veal, calf
**terrible** terrible
**testigo** *m.* witness
**tía** *f.* aunt
**tiempo** *m.* time
  **a . . .** in time
**tienda** *f.* store
**tierno,-a** tender
**tierra** *f.* earth
**tigre** *m.* tiger
**tijeras** *f.* scissors
**timbre** *m.* electric bell
**tinta** *f.* ink
**tintero** *m.* inkstand
**tinto** *m.* red (wine)
**tintorería** *f.* dyer's or
  cleaner's shop
**tío** *m.* uncle
**típico,-a** typical
**tipo** *m.* type
**toalla** *f.* towel
**tobillo** *m.* ankle
**tocador** *m.* dresser, boudoir
**tocante a** concerning
**tocar** to play (instrument), to
  ring, to knock on the door
**tocino** *m.* bacon
**todavía** yet
**todo** everything
**todos,-as** all
**tomate** *m.* tomato
**tomar** to take, to drink
**toreo** *m.* bullfight
**torero,-a** bullfighter

tormenta *f.* storm
toro *m.* bull
torrente *m.* torrent
tortilla *f.* omelet
tos *f.* cough
tostada *f.* toast
tostar to toast
total *m.* total
trabajador *m.* workman
trabajar to work
trabajo *m.* work
traducir to translate
traer to bring, to wear
tráfico *m.* traffic
traje *m.* suit
tranquilo,-a tranquil,
  peaceful
transacción *f.* transaction
transparente transparent
transportar to transport
tras behind
tratar (de) to try (to)
treinta thirty
tren *m.* train
tres three
trigo *m.* wheat
trimestre *m.* quarterly
  por . . . every three months
triste sad
trivial trivial
tropical tropical
trópico *m.* tropics
trucha *f.* trout
trueno *m.* thunder
turista *m.* tourist

# U

últimamente lately
último,-a last
ultramarino,-a ultramarine
uno one
un *m.;* una *f.* a, an
universal universal
universidad *f.* university
uno,-a one
unos *m.,* unas *f.* some
urgente urgent
usar to use

usted (usually abbreviated
  V., Vd., U., Ud.) you
ustedes you (pl.)
utilidad *f.* utility
uva *f.* grape

# V

vaca *f.* cow
vacación *f.* vacation
vacilar to hesitate
vainilla *f.* vanilla
vajilla dinnerware
valor *m.* value, bravery
vals *m.* waltz
vámonos let's go
vapor *m.* steamship, steam
varios,-as several
vaselina *f.* vaseline
vaso *m.* drinking glass
veces *f.* occasions, times
vecino,-a neighbor
vehículo *m.* vehicle
veinte twenty
vejez *f.* old age
velocidad *f.* speed
vender to sell
venir to come
ventana *f.* window
ventilador *m.* ventilator,
  electric fan
ventilar to ventilate
ventisca *f.* blizzard
ventura *f.* happiness, luck,
  chance
  por . . . by chance
ver to see
verano *m.* Summer
veras reality, truth
  ¿de . . . ? really?
verdad *f.* truth
  ¿no es . . . ? Is it not so?
  ¿es . . . ? Is it so?
  en . . . indeed
verde green
verse to appear, to look
vertical vertical
vestíbulo *m.* lobby
vestido *m.* dress
vestir to dress

**vestirse** to dress (yourself)
**vez** *f.* time
   **una . . .** once
   **tal . . .** maybe
**vía, una** one way
**viajar** to travel
**viaje** *m.* trip
**viajero-a** traveler
**vida** *f.* life
**viejo,-a** old
**vienés,-a** Viennese
**viento** *m.* wind
**viernes** *m.* Friday
**vinagre** *m.* vinegar
**vino** *m.* wine
**violeta** *f.* violet
**visita** *f.* visit
**visitar** to visit
**víspera** *f.* eve
**vista** *f.* view, sight
   **con . . . a** overlooking
**vistoso,-a** showy, beautiful
**vital** vital
**vitamina** *f.* vitamin

**¡Viva!** Hurrah!
**vitrina** *f.* shop window
**vivir** to live
**vocabulario** *m.* vocabulary
**volar** to fly
**volcar** to turn over, overturn
**voluntad** *f.* will
**volver** to return
**volverse** to become
**vuelo** *m.* flight

# Y

**y** and
**ya** already
**yegua** *f.* mare
**yerno** *m.* son-in-law
**yo** I
**yodo** *m.* iodine

# Z

**zanahoria** *f.* carrot
**zapatería** *f.* shoe store
**zapatilla** *f.* slipper
**zapato** *m.* shoe
**zorro** *m.* fox

# ENGLISH-SPANISH
# DICTIONARY

## A

a, an un, una
able, to be poder
above encima, arriba
absolutely absolutamente
accelerator acelerador m.
accident accidente m.
accidental accidental
accompany, to acompañar
according to según,
   conforme a
ache dolor m.
action acción f.
actor actor m.
actress actriz f.
address dirección f.
adjust, to ajustar
admirable admirable
adolescence adolescencia f.
advanced adelantado,-a
advertise, to anunciar
advertisement anuncio
aeronautic aeronáutico,-a
after después
against contra
age, old vejez f.
agency agencia f.
agent agente m.
agreeable agradable
agriculture agricultura f.
air aire m.
airmail correo aéreo
airplane aeroplano m.
   avión m.
airport aeropuerto m.
   puerto aéreo, m.
alas! ¡ay!
alcohol alcohol m.
alike conforme

all, todo,-a; todos,-as
allow me permítame
alone solo,-a
allow, to permitir, dejar
almond almendra f.
almost casi
already ya
also tambien
although aunque
always siempre
ambulance ambulancia f.
American americano,-a
among entre
amount importe m.
amusing gracioso
and y
angry enojado,-a
animal animal m.
ankle tobillo m.
announce, to anunciar
annual anual
any cuálquier
anyone cualquiera
answer, to contestar
answered contestado,-a
antenna antena f.
antiseptic antiséptico,-a
apartment departamento m.
aperitif aperitivo m.
appear, to parecer, verse
appetite apetito m.
applaud aplaudir
apple manzana f.
appointment cita f.;
   compromiso m.
appreciate, to apreciar
appreciation apreciación f.
apricot albaricoque m.
April abril m.
approve, to aprobar, celebrar

**archeology** arqueología f.
**architect** arquitecto m.
**architecture** arquitectura
**argue, to** discutir
**arm** brazo m.
**armchair** sillón m.
**aromatic** aromático,-a
**arrival** llegada f.
**arrive, to** llegar
**art** arte m.
**article** artículo m.
**artificial** artificial
**artist** artista m., f.
**artistic** artístico,-a
**artichoke** alcachofa f.
**as** como
**ash** ceniza f.
**ask, to** preguntar, pedir
**asparagus** espárrago m.
**aspirin** aspirina f.
**assistance** asistencia f.
**astringent** astringente m.
**at** a, en
**atomic** atómico,-a
**at once** ahora
**attend, to** asistir, atender
**attendance** asistencia f.
**attractive** atractivo,-a
**August** agosto m.
**aunt** tía
**authority** autoridad f.
**automobile** automóvil,
  auto m.
**autumn** otoño m.
**avenue** avenida f.
**aviation** aviación f.
**avoid, to** evadir
**away, to go** irse

# B

**back** espalda f.
**backward** atrasado,-a, atrás
**bacon** tocino m.
**bad** malo,-a
**badly** mal
**baggage** equipaje m.
**baggage check** talón m.
**balcony** balcón m.

**banana** plátano m.
**band** banda f.
**bank** banco m.
**bar** bar m.
**barley** cebada f.
**barometer** barómetro m.
**baseball** beisbol m.
**basket** canasta f.
**bath** baño m.
**bathe (yourself), to** bañarse
**bathroom** cuarto de baño
**bathtub** bañera f.
**battery** acumulador m.
**be, to** ser, estar, haber
**be careful!** ¡cuidado!
**beach** playa f.
**beans** fríjoles m.
**bear** oso m.
**beautiful** hermoso,-a
**beauty** hermosura
**beauty parlor** salón de belleza
**become, to** volverse
**bed** cama f.
**bedroom** dormitorio, m. alcoba f.
**bedspread** colcha f.
**beef** carne de res f.
**beefsteak** biftec m.
**been** estado
**beer** cerveza f.
**beet** remolacha f.
**before** delante, ante,
  antes de
**beg, to** rogar
**begin, to** comenzar
**begun** comenzado,-a
**behind** detrás, atrás
**believe, I** yo creo
**believe, to** creer
**bell (electric)** timbre m.
**below** abajo, debajo
**belt** cinturón m.
**beneath** debajo
**bet** apuesta f.
**bet, to** apostar
**better** mejor
**better, to get** mejorarse
**between** entre
**bicycle** bicicleta f.
**big** grande

bill cuenta *f.*
bird pájaro *m.*
birth nacimiento *m.*
bite, to morder
bitter amargo,-a
black negro,-a
blizzard ventisca *f.*
block cuadra *f.*
blond rubio,-a
blouse blusa *f.*
blue azul *m.*
blush, to ruborizarse
boarding house casa de
   huéspedes, pensión *f.*
boat barco *m.*
boil, to hervir
book libro *m.*
bookstore librería *f.*
boot bota *f.*
born, to be nacer
boss jefe, patrón *m.*
both ambos,-as
bother, to molestar
bottle botella *f.*
bought comprado,-a
box caja *f.*
box office taquilla *f.*
boy niño, muchacho *m.*
bracelet pulsera *f.*
brakes (automobile) frenos
brandy aguardiente *m.*
bravery valor *m.*
bread pan *m.*
break, to romper, quebrar
breakfast desayuno *m.*
breeze brisa *f.*
bridge puente *m.*
bring, to traer
broad ancho,-a
broiled asado,-a
brother hermano
brother-in-law cuñado *m.*
brown pardo
brunette moreno,-a
brush cepillo *m.*
brush, to cepillar
bucket balde *m.*
bud capullo *m.*
build, to construir

building edificio *m.*
bull toro *m.*
bullfight toreo *m.*
bullfighter torero,-a
bullring circo de toros *m.*
burn, to encender
bus autobús *m.*; camión *m.*
   (Mex.); guagua *f.* (Cub.)
business negocio *m.*
busy ocupado,-a
but pero, sino
butcher shop carnicería *f.*
butter mantequilla *f.*
button botón *m.*
buy, to comprar
   ... where can I ¿dónde
   puedo comprar?
by por
by means of mediante

# C

cabbage col *f.* repollo *m.*
cabin camarote *m.*
cabin, airplane cabina *f.*
cablegram cablegrama *m.*
cake ponqué *m.*
calendar calendario *m.*
calf becerro *m.*
call, to llamar
called, to be (name) llamarse
camera cámara *f.*
canary canario *m.*
cap gorra *f.*
car carro *m.*
carbon carbón *m.*
card tarjeta *f.*
cardinal cardinal
care, to take cuidar
carnation clavel
carnival carnaval *m.*
carrot zanahoria *f.*
carry, to llevar
cart driver carretero *m.*
cashier cajero,-a
cat gato,-a
catch, to coger
cathedral catedral *f.*
Catholic católico,-a
cattle ganado *m.*

**cauliflower** coliflor f.
**caution** cuidado
**celebrate, to** celebrar
**celebrity** celebridad f.
**celery** apio m.
**cent** centavo m.
**centigrade** centígrado
**central** central
**centuple** céntuplo
**century** siglo m.
**cereal** cereal m.
**certain** cierto,-a
**chair** silla f.
**chance, by** por ventura
**change** cambio m.
**change, to** cambiar
**character** carácter m.
**charm** gracia f.
**charming** simpático,-a
**cheap** barato,-a
**check** cheque m.
**check, restaurant** cuenta f.
**check, to** facturar
**cheese** queso m.
**cherry** cereza f.
**chest of drawers** cómoda f.
**chestnut** castaña f.
**chewing gum** chicle m.
**chicken** pollo m.
**child** niño,-a
**childhood** niñez f.
**Chinese** chino,-a
**chocolate** chocolate m.
**choose, to** seleccionar
**chops** chuletas f.pl.
**Christmas** Navidad f.
**Christmas Eve** Noche
  Buena f.
**church** iglesia f.
**cigar** cigarro puro m.
**cigarette** cigarrillo m.
**circular** circular
**city** ciudad f.
**city hall** ayuntamiento m.
**class** clase f.
**clean** limpio,-a
**clean, to** limpiar
**cleaner's shop** tintorería f.
**clearly** claro

**climate** clima m.
**climb, to** ascender
**clinic** clínica f.
**close** junto
**close, to** cerrar
**closed** cerrado,-a
**closet** armario
**cloth** paño m.
**clothes** ropa f.
**cloudy** nublado,-a
**club** casino, club m.
**clutch** embrague m.
**coal** carbón m.
**coast** costa f.
**coat** chaqueta f. saco m.
**cock** gallo m.
**cock fights** pelea de gallos f.
**cock pit** gallera f.
**cockroach** cucaracha f.
**cocktail** coctel m.
**cocoa** cacao m.
**cocoanut** coco m.
**coffee** café m.
  **... with milk** café con leche
  **... pot** cafetera f.
**cold, to get** enfriarse
**cold** frío,-a
**cold (illness)** resfrío, resfriado
**cold, I am** tengo frío
**cold, to catch** resfriarse
**collar** cuello m.
**colony** colonia f.
**color** color m.
**comb** peine m.
**come in, to** entrar
**come, to** venir
**come down, to** bajar
**comfortable** comfortable,
  cómodo,-a
**commercial** comercial
**company** compañía f.
**comparison** comparación f.
**complain, to** reclamar
**complaint** reclamación f.
**concern** firma f.
**concerning** acerca de,
  tocante a
**concert** concierto m.
**conductor** conductor m.

confetti confeti *m.*
congratulate, to congratular
consist, to consistir
construct, to construir
consultation consulta *f.*
contract, to contraer
contrary contrario,-a
convenient conveniente
conversation conversación *f.*
convince, to convencer
cook cocinero,-a
cook, to cocinar
cookie galleta *f.*
cool fresco,-a
copper cobre *m.*
copy copia *f.*
cordial cordial
corkscrew sacacorchos
corn maíz *m.*
   . . . ear of mazorca *f.*
corner esquina *f.*
correct correcto,-a
correction corrección *f.*
correspondence
   correspondencia *f.*
corridor corredor *m.*
cosmetic cosmético *m.*
cost, to costar
cotton algodón *m.*
cough tos *f.*
count, to contar
country campo, país *m.*
couple par *m.*
course, of por supuesto
courteous cortés
courtesy cortesía *f.*
cousin primo,-a
cover, to cubrir
cracker galleta *f.*
crazy loco,-a
cream crema *f.*
credential credencial *f.*
credit crédito *m.*
criminal criminal
cry, to llorar
crystal cristal *m.*
Cuban cubano,-a
cucumber pepino *m.*
cuff puño *m.*

cup taza *f.*
curtain cortina *f.*
custard natilla *f.*
cutlet filete *m.*
customhouse aduana *f.*
cut, to cortar

# D

daily diario *m.*
dance baile *m.*
dance, to bailar
danger peligro
dangerous peligroso,-a
dark oscuro-a
   to become . . . anochecer
darkness oscuridad *f.*
date (appointment) cita *f.,*
   compromiso *m.*
   (fruit) dátil *m.*
   (of calendar) fecha *f.*
daughter hija
day día *m.*
   . . . after tomorrow pasado
   mañana
   . . . before yesterday
   anteayer
daybreak amanecer *m.*
December diciembre *m.*
decide, to decidir
decision decisión *f.*
declaration declaración *f.*
decorate, to decorar
deduction deducción *f.*
deer ciervo *m.*
defect defecto *m.*
defective defectivo,-a
defend, to defender
degree grado *m.*
delicious delicioso,-a
deliver, to entregar
delivery entrega *f.*
demand, to exigir
dentist dentista *m.f.*
departure salida
deposit, to depositar
descend, to descender
describe, to describir
description descripción *f.*
desire deseo *m.;* gana *f.*

desk escritorio m.
dessert postre m.
detain, to detener
detest, to detestar
detour desvío m.
diamond diamante m.
dictionary diccionario m.
difference diferencia f.
different diferente
difficult difícil
difficulty dificultad f.
digestible digestible
digestion digestión f.
dine, to cenar
dining room comedor m.
direct directo,-a
direction dirección f.
director director,-a
dirty sucio,-a
directory directorio m.
dish plato m.
disagreeable desagradable
disappear, to desaparecer
disastrous desastroso,-a
discount descuento m.
discover, to descubrir
discuss, to discutir
discussion discusión f.
disobey, to desobedecer
distance distancia f.
distribute, to distribuír
divide, to dividir
dizziness mareo m.
doctor doctor,-a; médico,a
dog perro m.
dollar dólar m.
donkey burro,-a
door puerta f.
 . . . (car) portezuela f.
dot punto m.
double doble
doubt duda f.
doubt, to dudar
dove paloma f.
dozen docena f.
draft (financial) giro m.
 letra f.
 (current) corriente f.
dream sueño m.

dream, to soñar
dress vestido m.
dress, to vestir
dress (yourself), to vestirse
dressing (sauce) salsa f.
dressmaker modista f.
drink, to beber, tomar
drive, to manejar
driver conductor m
drugstore botica, droguería f.
drunk, to get emborracharse
dry, to (yourself) secarse
duck pato m.
dump, to echar
durable durable, duradero,-a
during durante
duty deber m.
 . . . (tax) impuesto m.

# E

each cada
eagle águila m.
ear oreja f.
earlier más temprano
early temprano
earth tierra f.
ease facilidad f.
east oriente m.
Easter Pascua f.
easy fácil
eat, to comer
effective efectivo,-a
egg huevo m.
 . . . fried huevo frito
 . . . hard boiled huevo duro
 . . . soft boiled huevo pasado
 por agua
eight ocho
eighteen dieciocho
eighty ochenta
elbow codo m.
electric eléctrico,-a
electricity electricidad f.
elegant elegante
elephant elefante m.
elevator elevador, ascensor m.
eleven once
embark, to embarcar
embroidery bordado m.

emergency emergencia *f.*
encounter encuentro *m.*
encounter, to encontrar
end fin *m.*
engineer ingeniero *m.*
enough bastante, suficiente
    ... that is basta
enter, to entrar
entertain, to entretener
entertainment diversión *f.*
enthusiasm entusiasmo *m.*
enthusiastic entusiástico
envelope cubierta *f.* sobre *m.*
equal igual
equivalent equivalente
errand mandado *m.*
error error *m.*
essential esencial
establish, to establecer
evade, to evadir
eve víspera *f.*
evening noche *f.*
everything todo
exact exacto,-a
exactly exactamente, en punto
exaggerate, to exagerar
exaggeration exageración *f.*
examine, to examinar
excavation excavación *f.*
except excepto, menos
excessive excesivo,-a
exchange cambio *m.*
excuse, to dispensar
    ... me excúseme,
      dispénseme
exhibition exhibición *f.*
existence existencia *f.*
exit salida
expensive caro,-a
expect, to esperar
expected esperado
experience experience *f.*
explain, to explicar
export, to exportar
express, to expresar
exterior exterior

**F**

fabric tela *f.*

face cara *f.*
facial facial
factory fábrica *f.*
fail, to fracasar
failure fracaso *m.*
fair justo,-a
fall, to caer
family familia *f.*
famous famoso,-a
fan aficionado,-a
far lejos
farm granja *f.*
farmer agricultor
fashion moda *f.*
fast pronto
fat gordo,-a
father padre *m.*
favor favor *m.*
favorite predilecto,-a
fear, to temer
fear miedo *m.*
feast festividad, fiesta *f.*
February, febrero *m.*
feel, to sentir
felt fieltro *m.*
fervor fervor
festival festival *m.*
fever fiebre *f.*
fifteen quince
fifty cincuenta *m.*
fig higo *m.*
film película *f.*
film roll rollo *m.*
finally finalmente, en fin
find, to encontrar
find out, to enterarse
finger dedo *m.*
finish, to terminar
finished terminado,-a
firm firma *f.*
first primero,-a
first class primera clase
fish pescado *m.*
fish, to pescar
fit, to ajustar
five cinco *m.*
fixed compuesto,-a
flame llama *f.*
flannel franela *f.*

**flight** vuelo *m.*
**float, to** flotar
**floor** piso *m.*
**flower** flor *f.*
**fly** mosco *m.*
**fly, to** volar
**food** alimento *m.*
**foot** pie *m.*
**for** para, por
**foreign** extranjero,-a
**foreigner** extranjero,-a
**forget, to** olvidar
**fork** tenedor *m.*
**form, to** formar
**formal** formal
**fort** fuerte *m.*
**fortune** fortuna *f.*
**forty** cuarenta
**forward** adelante
**fountain** fuente *f.*
**four** cuatro
**fourteen** catorce
**fox** zorro *m.*
**free** de balde, gratis
**freeze, to** helar
**French** francés,-sa
**frequently** frecuentemente
**fresh** fresco
**Friday** viernes *m.*
**fried** frito,-a
**friend** amigo,-a
**frightened, to get** asustarse
**from** desde, de
**front, in** al frente
**frost** helada *f.*
**frozen** congelado,-a
**fruit** fruta *f.*
**fry, to** freír
**funeral** funeral *m.*
**funny** chistoso,-a
**fur** piel *f.*
**furnished** amueblado,-a
**furniture** mobiliario *m.*

# G

**gamble, to** jugar
**game** juego *m.*
**garage** garage *m.*
**garden** jardín *m.*

**gardener** hortelano,-a
**garlic** ajo *m.*
**gas station** estación de
    gasolina *f.*
**gasoline** gasolina *f.*
**general** general *m.*
**generator** generador *m.*
**gentleman** señor, caballero
**get rid of, to** deshacerse
**get off or down, to** bajar
**gin** ginebra *f.*
**girl** niña, muchacha
**give, to** dar
    dé (imp.)
    ... it to me démelo
**glad, to be** alegrarse
**glove** guante *m.*
**go, to** ir
    ... in, to entrar
    ... to bed, to acostarse
    ... down to descender
    let's ... vámonos
**goat** cabra *f.*
**God** Dios
**gold** oro *m.*
**golf** golf *m.*
**good** bueno,-a; buen
    ... afternoon buenas tardes
    ... luck buena suerte
    ... morning buenos días
    ... night buenas noches
**goods** artículos
**goose** ganso *m.*
**government** gobierno *m.*
**graceful** gracioso,-a
**gracious!** ¡caramba!
**grain** grano *m.*
**granddaughter** nieta *f.*
**grandfather** abuelo *m.*
**grandmother** abuela *f.*
**grandson** nieto *m.*
**grape** uva *f.*
**gray** gris *m.*
**green** verde
**greet, to** saludar
**greeting** saludo *m.*
**groan** quejido *m.*
**gross** gruesa *f.*
**ground** suelo *m.*

**ground floor** piso bajo
**grow, to** crecer
**growth** crecimiento *m.*
**guest** invitado,-a
**guitar** guitarra *f.*

# H

**hair** pelo *m.*
**half** medio,-a, mitad
**hall** corredor *m.*
**ham** jamón *m.*
**hand** mano *f.*
**hand (of a watch)**
    manecilla *f.*
**handbag** cartera *f.*
**handkerchief** pañuelo *m.*
**handsome** guapo,-a
**happiness** felicidad,
    ventura *f.*
**happy** contento,-a
**hard** duro,-a
**hare** liebre *f.*
**harvest** cosecha *f.*
**haste** prisa *f.*
**hat** sombrero *m.*
**hat store** sombrerería *f.*
**hate, to** odiar
**hatred** odio *m.*
**have, to** tener
**hay** heno *m.*
**hazelnut** avellana *f.*
**he** él
**head** cabeza *f.*
**health** salud *f.*
**hear, to** oír
**hearing** oído *m.*
**heat** calor *m.*
**heating** calefacción *f.*
**heel** tacón *m.*
**hen** gallina *f.*
**here** aquí
**hiccough** hipo *m.*
**high** alto,-a; elevado,-a
**highway** carretera *f.*
**hire, to** alquilar
**history** historia *f.*
**holiday** fiesta, *f.*
**home** hogar *m.*
**honey** miel de abejas

**honeymoon** luna de miel *f.*
**honor** honor *m.*
**hope** esperanza *f.*
**hope, to** esperar
**horse** caballo *m.*
**horse race** carrera de caballos
**hospital** hospital *m.*
**hospitality** hospitalidad *f.*
**hot** caliente
    ...**I am** tengo calor
**hour** hora *f.*
**house** casa *f.*
**how** cómo
    ...**are you?**
        ¿cómo está usted?
    ...**far is it?**
        ¿Qué tan lejos es?
    ...**many** cuántos
    ...**much** cuánto
**humidity** humedad *f.*
**humor** humor *m.*
**hundred** ciento
**hunger** hambre *m.*
**hungry, I am** tengo hambre
**hurry, to** apurarse
    ...**up!** ¡apúrese!
**hurt, to** doler
    ...**yourself, to** lastimarse
**husband** esposo, marido *m.*

# I

**I** yo
**ice** hielo *m.*
**ice cream** helado *m.*
**idea** idea *f.*
**if** si
**ignorance** ignorancia *f.*
**ignorant** ignorante
**ill** mal
    **very**... grave
**illegal** ilegal
**illustration** ilustración *f.*
**imagination** imaginación *f.*
**imitation** imitación *f.*
**immense** inmenso,-a
**impatience** impaciencia *f.*
**import, to** importar
**important** importante
**impossible** imposible

**impossibility** imposibilidad *f.*
**in** en
**incidentally** por cierto
**include, to** incluír
**income** renta *f.*
**incompetent** incompetente
**incorrect** incorrecto,-a
**indeed** en verdad
**independence**
  independencia *f.*
**indigestion** indigestión *f.*
**indisposed** indispuesto,-a
**industrial** industrial
**infection** infección *f.*
**influence** influencia *f.*
**inform, to** informar
**inhabitant** habitante
**initial** inicial
**ink** tinta *f.*
**inoculate, to** inocular
**insect** insecto *m.*
**inside** adentro, dentro
**install, to** instalar
**instant** instante *m.*
**insult** insulto *m.*
**insurance** seguro
**intelligent** inteligente
**interior** interior
**international** internacional
**interrupt, to** interrumpir
**intimate** íntimo,-a
**introduce, to** presentar
**introduction** introducción
**invitation** invitación *f.*
**invite, to** invitar
**invoice** factura *f.*
**iron, to** planchar
**is** es
**it is** es
**itinerary** itinerario *m.*

**J**

**jacket** chaqueta *f.*
**jail** cárcel *f.*
**jam (tight spot)** aprieto
**January** enero *m.*
**jealousy** celos *m.*
**jest** burla *f.*
**jewel** joya *f.*

**jewelry store** joyería *f.*
**Jewish** judío
**joke** chiste *m.*
**journal** diario *m.*
**joy** gozo *m.*
**judgment** juicio *m.*
**juice** jugo *m.*
**July** julio *m.*
**jump, to** saltar
**June** junio *m.*
**just** justo,-a
**justice** justicia *f.*

**K**

**keep out!** prohibida la
  entrada!
**key** llave *f.*
**kilogram** kilo *m.*
**kind** clase *f.*
**kitchen** cocina *f.*
**knife** cuchillo *m.*
**knock on the door, to** tocar
**know, to** saber
**know, to (people, places)**
  conocer

**L**

**laborious** laborioso,-a
**lace** encaje *m.*
**lack, to** faltar
**ladder** escalera *f.*
**lake** lago *m.*
**lamb** cordero *m.*
**lamp** lámpara *f.*
**lamp shade** pantalla *f.*
**language** idioma *m.*
**large** grande
**lark** alondra *f.*
**last** último,-a; postrero,-a
  ...**night** anoche
  **at**... al fin, por fin
  **to**... durar
**lately** últimamente
**later** más tarde, luego
**laugh, to** reír
**laughter** risa *f.*
**laughter, burst of** carcajada
**laundry** lavandería *f.*
**lavatory** baño *m.*

lawyer abogado *m.*
lazy perezoso,-a
leaf hoja *f.*
learn, to aprender
lease, to arrendar
leather piel *f.*
leave, to dejar, salir
left izquierda *f.*
leg pierna *f.*
legal legal
lemon limón *m.*
lemonade limonada *f.*
lend, to prestar
lentil lenteja *f.*
less menos
lesson lección *f.*
let, to dejar
letter carta, letra *f.*
lettuce lechuga *f.*
library biblioteca *f.*
lie mentira *f.*
lie, to mentir
lie down, to acostar
life vida *f.*
lift, to levantar
light luz *f.*
light, to encender
lightning relámpago *m.*
like, to gustar
lily lirio *m.*
lime lima *f.*
linen lino *m.*
lion león *m.*
list lista *f.*
listen! ¡oíga!
little poco,-a; menudo,-a;
   chiquito,-a
live, to vivir
living room sala *f.*
lobby vestíbulo *m.*
local local
location sitio *m.*
lock in, to encerrar
locker gaveta *f.*
long largo,-a
   ... too muy largo,-a
look! ¡míre!
lose, to perder
lottery lotería *f.*

loud alto,-a
love amor *m.*
love, to querer
low bajo,-a
lubrication lubricación *f.*
lubricant lubricante *m.*
lubricate, to lubricar
luck suerte *f.*
lunch almuerzo *m.*
lunch (to have) almorzar
luxury lujo *m.*

# M

machine máquina *f.*
machinery maquinaria *f.*
maid criada *f.*
maid, room camarera *f.*
mail correo *m.*
mailbox buzón *m.*
major mayor
make, to hacer, realizar
man hombre
manage, to manejar
manner modo *m.*
mansion mansión *f.*
many muchos,-as
many, as, so tantos, as
map mapa *m.*
March marzo *m.*
market plaza *f.*
market place mercado *m.*
marmalade mermelada *f.*
match fósforo *m.*
mattress colchón *m.*
May mayo *m.*
maybe tal vez
mayor alcalde *m.*
me mí
measure, to medir
meat carne *f.*
mechanic mecánico,-a
medicine medicina *f.*
meet, to encontrar
melon melón *m.*
melt, to derretir
memory memoria *f.*
mend, to remendar
menu menú *m.*
merchandise mercancía *f.*

merchant comerciante *m.*
metal metal *m.*
Mexican mexicano,-a
midday mediodía *m.*
middle medio *m.*
midnight medianoche *f.*
milk leche *f.*
mine mío,-a
mine mina, *f.*
mineral mineral *m.*
minute minuto *m.*
mistake, to make a
    equivocarse
mix, to revolver
modern moderno,-a
moment momento *m.*
Monday lunes *m.*
money dinero *m.*
    paper ... billete
monkey mono *m.*
month mes *m.*
moon luna *f.*
more más
morning mañana *f.*
moreover además
mother madre
motor motor *m.*
motorist motorista *m., f.*
mouse ratón *m.*
move, to mudar, mover
movie screen pantalla *f.*
moving moviendo
moving picture película *f.*
much mucho,-a
much, as, so tanto,-a
    too ... demasiado
mud lodo, fango *m.*
mule mula *f.*
municipal municipal
mural mural
museum museo *m.*
mushroom seta *f.*
music música *f.*
mustard mostaza *f.*
mutton carnero *m.*
my mi, mis
myself mí

# N

name nombre *m.*
napkin servilleta *f.*
narrow estrecho, angosto,-a
nation nación *f.*
national nacional
nationality nacionalidad *f.*
native nativo,-a
natural natural
naturally naturalmente
navy marina *f.*
near cerca, junto
    ... to cerca de
necessary necesario,-a
necessity necesidad *f.*
neck cuello *m.*
necktie corbata *f.*
need, to necesitar
needle aguja *f.*
needlework costura *f.*
negative negativo
negligent negligente
neighbor vecino,-a
neither ningún, ninguno,-a
    tampoco, ni
nephew sobrino *m.*
nervous nervioso,-a
never nunca, jamás
new nuevo,-a
New Year Año Nuevo
news noticias *f.*
newspaper periódico *m.*
newsreel noticiario *m.*
next próximo,-a
niece sobrina *f.*
night noche *f.*
nine nueve *m.*
ninety noventa
nineteen diecinueve
no no
noble noble
nobody nadie
noon mediodía *m.*
no one ninguno,-a
nor ni
north norte
North America Norte
    América

North American
  norteamericano,-a
note nota *f.*
notebook cuaderno *m.*
note, to notar
notice, to notar
nothing nada
November noviembre *m.*
now ahora
  right ... ahora
number número *m.*
numerous numeroso,-a
nut nuez *f.*

## O

oat avena *f.*
obtain, to obtener
occasion ocasión *f.*
occupation ocupación *f.*
occupy, to ocupar
October octubre *m.*
occur, to ocurrir
oculist oculista *m.*
odd raro,-a
of de
offend, to ofender
offended ofendido,-a
offensive ofensivo,-a
offer, to ofrecer
office oficina *f.*
official oficial
often a menudo
oil aceite *m.*
old viejo,-a
olive aceituna *f.*
omelet tortilla *f.*
on en, sobre
once una vez
one uno,-a
one way una vía
onion cebolla *f.*
open abierto,-a
open, to abrir
opera ópera *f.*
operation operación *f.*
operator operador
opinion opinión *f.*
opposite al frente
or o

orange naranja *f.*
  ... juice jugo de naranja
orchard huerta *f.*
orchestra orquesta *f.*
orchid orquídea *f.*
order orden *f.*
order, to pedir
ordinarily generalmente
ordinary ordinario,-a
original original
ornament adorno *m.*
other otro,-a
ounce onza *f.*
our, ours nuestro,-a
ourselves nosotros,-as
out of order descompuesto,-a
outside exterior, fuera, afuera,
oven horno *m.*
overcoat abrigo *m.*
overturn, to volcar
own propio,-a
owner dueño,-a
ox buey
oyster ostra *f.*

## P

park, to estacionar
parrot loro *m.*
patience paciencia *f.*
patient paciente
patriotic patriótico,-a
pattern patrón *m.*
package paquete *m.*
paint, to pintar
painting pintura *f.*
pair par *m.*
palace palacio *m.*
palm tree palma, palmera *f.*
paper papel *m.*
park parque *m.*
parking parqueadero *m.*
pass, to pasar
past pasado,-a
paste pasta *f.*
pay, to pagar
payment pago *m.*
peaceful tranquilo,-a
peach melocotón *m.*
pear pera *f.*

**peas** guisantes *m.*
**peasant** peón *m.*
**pen** pluma *f.*
**pencil** lápiz *m.*
**penicillin** penicilina *f.*
**pension** pensión *f.*
**people** gente *f.*
**pepper** pimienta *f.*
**per cent** por ciento
**percentage** tanto por ciento
**perfect** perfecto,-a
**perform, to** realizar
**perfume** perfume *m.*
**perhaps** quizá, quizás, acaso
**permanent** permanente *f.*
**permanent wave** permanente
**permitted** permitido,-a
**person, in** personalmente
**personal** personal
**personally** personalmente
**perspire, to** sudar
**persuade, to** persuadir
**peso** peso *m.*
**petroleum** petróleo *m.*
**phonograph** fonógrafo *f.*
**phonograph record** disco *m.*
**photograph** fotografía *f.*
**photograph, to** fotografiar
**pick up, to** levantar
**picture** pintura *f.*
    cuadro *m.*
    retrato (portrait) *m.*
**pie** pastel *m.*
**pier** muelle *m.*
**pig** cerdo *m.*
**pill** píldora *f.*
**pillow** almohada *f.*
**pilot** piloto *m.*
**pine tree** pino *m.*
**pineapple** piña *f.*
**pipe** pipa *f.*
**pitcher** jarra *f.*
**place** sitio, lugar *m.*
**plan** plan *m.*
**plant** planta *f.*
**plate** plato *m.*
**platter** fuente *f.*
**play, to** jugar
**play, to (instrument)** tocar

**pleasant** agradable
**pleasure** gusto, placer *m.*
**plum** ciruela *f.*
**pocket** bolsillo *m.*
**point** punto *m.*
**point, to** señalar
**policeman** policía *m.*
**politics** política *f.*
**poor** pobre
**popular** popular
**poppy** amapola *f.*
**pork** puerco *m.*
   ... **chop** chuleta de cerdo
**port** puerto *m.*
**position** posición *f.*
**positive** positivo,-a
**possible** posible
**possibly** posiblemente
**postal** postal
**potato** papa *f.*
**pour, to** echar
**powder** polvo *m.*
    polvos (cosmetic)
**practice, to** practicar
**practical** práctico,-a
**precious** precioso,-a
**prefer, to** preferir
**preferred** predilecto,-a
**prepare, to** preparar
**prescription** receta *f.*
**present** presente, regalo (gift) *m.*
**present, to** presentar
**pretty** bonito,-a
**price** precio *m.*
**principal** principal
**print, to** imprimir
**prize** premio *m.*
**probably** probablemente
**proceed, to** proceder
**produce, to** producir
**product** producto *m.*
**profession** profesión *f.*
**profit** ganancia *f.*
**program** programa *m.*
**progress** progreso *m.*
**progress, to** progresar
**prohibit, to** prohibir
**promise, to** prometer
**pronounce, to** pronunciar

pronunciation
   pronunciación f.
proof prueba f.
propeller hélice f.
proper propio,-a
protest, to protestar
protection protección f.
Protestant protestante
prove, to probar
province provincia f.
public público,-a
pulse pulso m.
pumpkin calabaza f.
punctual puntual
purchase compra f.
purse bolso,-a
put, to poner
   ... on, to ponerse
   ... to bed, to acostar
   ... out, to apagar, echar

## Q

quantity cantidad f.
quarter cuarto m.
quarterly trimestre
question pregunta f.
quick aprisa
quotation cotización f.

## R

rabbit conejo m.
racial racial
radiator radiador m.
radio radio m.
radish rábano m.
railroad ferrocarril m.
railroad car coche m.
rain lluvia f.
rain, to llover
raincoat impermeable m.;
   gabardina f.
raise, to levantar, alzar
raisin pasa f.
ranch rancho m.
rapid rápido,-a
rapidly rápidamente
rare raro,-a
raspberry frambuesa f.
rat rata f.

raw crudo,-a
rayon rayón m.
razor navaja de afeitar
razor blade cuchilla f.
read, to leer
ready listo,-a
reality realidad, verdad f.
realize, to realizar
really? ¿de veras?
reason razón f.
receipt recibo m.
receive, to recibir
recent reciente
recognize, to reconocer
recommend, to recomendar
recommendation
   recomendación f.
recreation recreación f.
red colorado, rojo,-a
red snapper pargo m.,
   huachinango m. (Mex.)
reduce, to reducir
reflector reflector m.
refresh, to refrescar
refrigeration refrigeración f.
refrigerator refrigeradora f.
region región f.
register, to registrar,
   matricular
registration registración,
   matriculación f.
regularity regularidad f.
relation relación f.
relative pariente, m.
remain, to quedarse
remember, to recordar
remind, to acordar
rent renta f.
rent, to arrendar
repair, to componer
repeat, to repetir
repair, to reparar
require, to requerir
resemble, to parecerse
residential residencial
respectable respetable
responsible responsable
rest, to descansar
restaurant restaurante m.

**restriction** restricción *f.*
**return, to** regresar, devolver, volver
**reunion** reunión *f.*
**rib** costilla *f.*
**ribbon** cinta *f.*
**rice** arroz *m.*
**ride, to** montar
**ride, to take a** pasear
**ridiculous** ridículo,-a
**right** derecha *f.* (direction), correcto
**rise, to** ascender, subir
**river** río *m.*
**road** camino *m.*
**roadmap** guía del viajero
**roast, to** asar
**roast beef** rosbif *m.*
**roasted** asado,-a
**rob, to** robar
**robbery** robo *m.*
**romantic** romántico,-a
**room** pieza, habitación, *f.;* cuarto, *m.*
**roomy** espacioso,-a
**rosary** rosario *m.*
**rose** rosa *f.*
**route** ruta *f.*
**rubber** goma, caucho
**rug** alfombra *f.*
**rum** ron *m.*
**rumba** rumba *f.*
**rural** rural
**rumor** rumor *m.*
**Russian** ruso,-a
**rye** centeno *m.*

## S

**sail, to** embarcar
**safe** seguro,-a
**salad** ensalada *f.*
**salary** salario *m.*
**salt** sal *f.*
**salty** salado,-a
**same** mismo,-a
**sample** muestra *f.*
**sandwich** sandwich *m.*
**sardine** sardina *f.*
**satisfy, to** satisfacer

**Saturday** sábado *m.*
**sauce** salsa *f.*
**save, to** salvar
**say, to** decir
**scarcely** apenas
**school** colegio *m.;* escuela *f.*
**scissors** tijeras *f.*
**scorpion** alacrán *m.*
**scrape** lío *m.*
**scratch, to** rascar
**scream** grito *m.*
**scream, to** gritar
**sculpture** escultura *f.*
**seal** sello *m.*
**seasick, to get** marearse
**season** estación *f.*
**seat** asiento *m.*
**second** segundo,-a
**second class** segunda clase
**secretary** secretario,-a
**section** sección *f.*
**sedative** sedativo *m.*
**see, to** ver
**seem, to** parecer
**seldom** rara vez
**select, to** seleccionar
**selection** selección *f.*
**self starter** arranque automático *m.*
**sell, to** vender
**send, to** mandar
**sensation** sensación *f.*
**September** septiembre *m.*
**serve, to** servir
**service** servicio *m.*
**seven** siete
**seventeen** diecisiete
**seventy** setenta
**several** varios,-as
**sew, to** coser
**shade** sombra *f.*
**shave, to** afeitar
**she** ella
**sheep** oveja *f.*
**sheet** sábana, hoja *f.*
**shepherd** pastor *m.*
**shipment** despacho, envío, *m.*
**shirt** camisa *f.*
**shoe** zapato *m.*

shoestore zapatería f.
shop almacén m.
short corto,-a
   too ... muy corto,-a
shoulder hombro m.
shout, to gritar
shovel pala f.
show, to enseñar, mostrar, señalar
shrimp camarón m.
shut, to cerrar
sick enfermo,-a
   I am ... estoy enfermo
sickness enfermedad f.
get sick, to enfermarse
sidewalk acera f.
sigh suspiro m.
sight vista f.
sign, to firmar
sign letrero m.
silence silencio m.
silk seda f.
simple simple
simplicity simplicidad f.
since desde, pues
sincerity sinceridad f.
sing, to cantar
single solo, simple, único
sink fregadero m.
sister hermana f.
sister-in-law cuñada f.
sit, to sentar
sit down, to sentarse
situate, to situar
situation situación f.
six seis
sixteen dieciséis m.
sixty sesenta
size talla f.
sky cielo m.
sleep, to dormir
sleep, to go to dormirse
sleeve manga f.
slip, to resbalar
slipper zapatilla f.
slow despacio, lento
small pequeño, chiquito,-a
   too... muy pequeño,-a; muy chiquito,-a

smell, to oler
smile, to sonreír
smoke, to fumar
sneeze estornudo m.
snore, to roncar
snow nieve f.
snow, to nevar
so (thus) así
   ... long hasta luego
   ... that conque
soap jabón m.
soap dish jabonera f.
sob sollozo m.
sociable sociable
social social
society sociedad f.
sock calcetín m.
sofa sofá m.
soft suave, blando,-a
soft drink bebida gaseosa
sole suela f.
solution solución f.
some unos,-as
somebody alguien
someone alguno,-a
something algo
son hijo
song canto m.; canción f.
soon pronto
sorry, to be sentir
   I am ... lo siento
soup sopa f.
south sur m.
South America Sur América
souvenir recuerdo
sow, to sembrar
sowing siembra
space espacio m.
spacious espacioso,-a
Spain España f.
Spaniard español,-a
Spanish español,-a
spark plug bujía f.
sparrow gorrión m.
speak, to hablar
special especial
specially especialmente
speech discurso m.
speed velocidad f.

spicy picante
spinach espinaca f.
sponge esponja f.
spoon cuchara f.
spoonful cucharada f.
spring primavera f.
square plaza f.; cuadrado,-a
squirrel ardilla f.
stadium estadio m.
staircase escalera f.
stairs escalones m.
stamp sello m.; estampilla f.
stand up, to pararse
state estado m.
station estación f.
station wagon camioneta f.
stationery store papelería f.
statue estatua f.
stay, to quedarse
steak bisté m.
steal, to robar
steam vapor m.
steamship vapor m.
steps escalones m.
stew guisado m.
stockings medias f. pl.
stomach estómago m.
stone piedra f.
stop! ¡pare!, ¡alto!
stop, to parar
store tienda f.
storm tormenta f.
story cuento m.
stove estufa f.
straight, straight ahead
  derecho,-a
strange extraño,-a
straw paja f.
strawberry fresa f.
street calle f.
string bean ejote m.
student estudiante
stupid estúpido,-a
style moda f.; estilo m.
suburb suburbio m.
success éxito m.
successively sucesivamente
sudden de pronto, de repente
sufficient suficiente, bastante

sugar azúcar m.
sugar bowl azucarero m.
suit traje m.
suitcase maleta f.
summer verano m.
sun sol m.
Sunday domingo m.
supper cena f.
supper, to have cenar
supposed supuesto
sure cierto,-a
surprise, to sorprender
swallow golondrina f.
sweater suéter m.
sweep, to barrer
sweet dulce
sweet potato batata f.
swim, to nadar
swimming pool piscina f.
system sistema m.

## T

table mesa f.
tablecloth mantel m.
tailor sastre m.
tailor shop sastrería f.
take, to llevar, tomar
take leave, to despedirse
tall alto,-a
tango tango m.
tank tanque m.
tassel espiga f.
taste gusto m.
taste, to probar, gustar
tasteless desabrido,-a
tea té m.
teach, to enseñar
teacher maestro,-a
tear lágrima f.
tear, to romper
teaspoon cucharita f.
telegram telegrama m.
telegraph operator telegrafista
telephone teléfono m.
television televisión f.
tell, to decir
  ...me dígame
temper genio m.

temperature fiebre,
  temperatura *f.*
ten diez *m.*
tender tierno,-a
tenth décimo,-a
terrace terraza *f.*
terrible terrible
test, to probar
thank you gracias
that ese, eso,-a, aquel,-la, que,
  quien, cual
that way por allá
the el, la, los, las
  about ... del
  at ... al
  from ... del
  of ... del
  to ... al
theft robo *m.*
then entonces, luego
there ahí, allí, allá
  ... is, are hay
these estos, estas
thin delgado,-a
thing cosa *f.*
think, I yo creo, yo pienso
think, to creer, pensar
third, one tercio
thirsty, I am tengo sed
thirteen trece
thirty treinta
this este, esta
  ... one éste, ésta
  ... way por aquí
thought pensamiento *m.*
thousand mil
thread hilo *m.*
three tres
thunder trueno *m.*
Thursday jueves *m.*
ticket boleto, billete,
  pasaje *m.*
tidy aseado,-a
tiger tigre *m.*
tight apretado estrecho,-a
tile mosaico *m.*
time tiempo, vez
  in, on ... a tiempo
  to have a good ... divertirse

times veces
tire llanta *f.*
tired cansado,-a
timetable itinerario,
  horario
tin estaño *m.*
tip propina *f.*
tired, to get cansarse
to para, a
toast tostada *f.*
toast, to tostar
tobacco tabaco *m.*
today hoy
together juntos,-as
tomato tomate *m.*
tomorrow mañana *f.*
tongue lengua *f.*
tonight esta noche
tooth diente *m.*
toothbrush cepillo de dientes
torrent torrente *m.*
toss, to echar
total total *m.*
touch, to tocar
tourist turista, viajero
toward hacia
towel toalla *f.*
town pueblo *m.*
toy juguete *m.*
traffic tráfico *m.*
train tren *m.*
transaction transacción *f.*
translate, to traducir
transparent transparente
transport, to transportar
travel, to viajar
traveler viajero,-a
travelers check cheque de viajero
tray bandeja *f.*
tree árbol *m.*
trimming adorno *m.*
trip viaje *m.*
trivial trivial
tropical tropical
tropics trópico *m.*
trouble dificultad *f.*; lío *m.*
trousers pantalones *m.*
trout trucha *f.*
truck camión *m.*

trunk baúl *m.*
truth veras, verdad *f.*
try it on mídaselo
try to, to tratar de
Tuesday martes *m.*
turkey pavo *m.*
turn off the light, to apagar
turn over, to volcar
turnip nabo *m.*
twelve doce
twenty veinte
twenty-five veinticinco
two dos
throw, to echar
type tipo *m.*
typewriter máquina de
   escribir
typical típico,-a

## U

ugliness fealdad *f.*
ugly feo,-a
ultramarine ultramarino,-a
umbrella paraguas *m.*
uncertainty duda *f.*
uncle tío *m.*
under debajo, bajo
undershirt camiseta *f.*
understand, to comprender,
   entender
underwear ropa interior
undress, to desvestirse
until hasta
   . . . we meet again hasta la
   vista
unwrap, to desenvolver
up to hasta
up, to go subir
upon sobre
urgent urgente
us nos, nosotros,-as
used to be era
utility utilidad *f.*

## V

vain, in en balde
value valor, importe *m.*
vaseline vaselina *f.*
veal ternera *f.*

vegetable legumbre *f.*
vehicle vehículo *m.*
velvet terciopelo *m.*
ventilate, to ventilar
ventilator ventilador *m.*
vertical vertical
very muy
   . . . well muy bien
vest chaleco *m.*
Viennese vienés,-a
view vista *f.*
vinegar vinagre *m.*
violet violeta *f.*
visit visita *f.*
visit, to visitar
vitamin vitamina *f.*
vocabulary vocabulario *m.*

## W

wage pago, sueldo, jornal
waist cintura, talle *m.*
waistline cintura *f.*
wait, to esperar
waited esperado
waiter camarero,-a
wake up, to despertar
walk, to caminar, andar
walk, to take a pasear,
   caminar
wall pared *f.*
wallet cartera
waltz vals *m.*
want, to querer
warm caloroso, caliente
was era
was, there había, hubo
wash basin lavabo *m.*
wash, to lavar
   . . . to (yourself) bañarse
watch reloj
watchmaker relojero *m.*
watch shop relojería *f.*
water agua *m.*
watermelon sandía *f.*
waterproof impermeable *m.*
wave ola *f.*
we nosotros,-as
weakness debilidad *f.*
wear, to llevar

Wednesday miércoles *m.*
week semana *f.*
  by the ... por semana
weight peso *m.*
weigh, to pesar
weigh, to (yourself) pesarse
well bien
  ... done bien asado
were era
were, there había, hubo
west occidente *m.*
West Indies Antillas
what? ¿qué?
whatever cualquiera
wheat trigo m.
wheel rueda *f.*
when cuando
whenever siempre que
where donde
which que, cuál,-es
whip látigo *m.*
white blanco,-a
who? ¿quién?
whoever quienquiera
wide amplio, ancho,-a
wife esposa *f.*
will voluntad *f.*
wind viento *m.*
window ventana *f.*
windshield parabrisa *m.*
windshield wiper
  limpiavidrios
wine vino *m.*
winter invierno *m.*
wish, to desear
with con
with me conmigo

within dentro de
without sin, fuera
witness testigo *m.*
wolf lobo *m.*
woman mujer
wonderful admirable
wood madera *f.*
woods bosque *m.*
wool lana *f.*
word palabra *f.*
work trabajo *m.*
work, to trabajar
workman trabajador
world mundo *m.*
worried preocupado,-a
worry, to preocupar
worse peor
wrap, to envolver
wrapped envuelto,-a
wrinkle arruga *f.*
write, to escribir
writing escribiendo
written escrito

# Y

yawn bostezo *m.*
year año *m.*
yellow amarillo,-a
yes sí
yesterday ayer
yet todavía, aun
young joven
youth juventud *f.*

# Z

zero cero *m.*